DOUCHEBAGS TO DIAMONDS

Douchebags to Diamonds

HOW TO TAKE CHARGE OF YOUR LOVE LIFE AND ATTRACT MR. RIGHT

STACEY DEWALD

Paperback ISBN: 978-1-7376293-0-6
Hardcover ISBN: 978-1-7376293-1-3
eBook ISBN: 978-1-7376293-2-0

Cover and Interior Design: Danna Mathias Steele
Cover Photo: Nikki Closser
1st edition, January 2022
Printed in the United States of America

For my daughter, Jaide.

Acknowledgments

I offer deep appreciation to my loving, intuitive, and gifted ghostwriter, Dr. Cindy Childress, for bringing my book to life, as well as my talented graphic designer, Danna Mathias, for designing the cover and the interior, and my skilled team of copy editors, Lesley-Anne Longo and Anna Krusinski.

A special thank you to you, my reader, for choosing my book to read. I hope you feel all the love, support, and healing energy I put into each page.

In addition, I would like to thank my amazing husband, Chris, for his unconditional love and support. Thank you to my daughter, Jaide, for encouraging me to write this book and believing in me every step of the way, and my stepdaughter, Shay, for her enthusiasm. Thank you to my parents, Steve and Nancy, for being two of my biggest fans and supporters. To my sister from another mister, Amber, thank you for not letting me give up. And to every girlfriend who has stood by my side, I adore you.

Contents

Your task is not to seek for love,
but merely to seek and find all the barriers
within yourself that you have built against it.

—RUMI

Introduction

My boyfriend, Chris and I were on a helicopter ride over Whistler, British Columbia. The snow-topped mountains were beautiful, even if we couldn't really talk over the sound of the spinning blades. As I understood it, our plan was to land on a glacier and have champagne, but the pilot was having trouble landing. We circled the area three times, and by then I was starting to get dizzy and was ready to head back to the lodge. I was just about to tell the pilot to take us back when Chris pulled a little black box out of his pocket.

"Will you marry me?" he asked. I had to read his lips over the noise.

"Yes!" I exclaimed. The proposal may not have been as perfect as he'd planned, but it was perfect in my eyes, and he truly is my Mr. Right.

He respects his mom, is kind to his ex-wife, loves my daughter as if she were his own, and, most of all, is the exact opposite of a douchebag.

If you're reading this and just threw up a little in your mouth, I don't blame you. Before you roll your eyes (if you haven't already), I want you to know that my dating life wasn't always this fabulous.

For most of my adult life, I didn't think guys like Chris existed— and that even if they did, they would never be interested in someone as broken and unlovable as myself.

How do you release years of shame? You give it a voice.

This is my story.

We all have patterns that appear again and again in our lives, patterns that we don't like, and that leave us feeling insecure, powerless, defeated, and even inadequate at times. We tend to blame these patterns on an external source, such as the person we're dating, or our spouse, our ex, our parents, our boss, our friends, or even our children. But the truth is, we created these patterns ourselves, and we're the only ones who can break them.

For me, the pattern I was stuck in for years was toxic relationships, and I mean *toxic*. (To be fair, these guys weren't all terrible, but I had a bad habit of pushing the nice guys away.)

To give you an idea, here are a few examples of my past dating experiences:

- One boyfriend used to put me down whenever I ate. He'd say things like, "You're hungry again?" or "Are you really going to eat that?"
- One guy told me that his parents died in a car accident when he was young, only for me to eventually find out that his parents were very much still alive, and he just didn't have a relationship with them.
- I've been with a guy who was a serial cheater who stalked me, broke into my home, and tapped my phone after I broke up with him.
- After confronting another boyfriend about his excessive drinking, he grabbed me by the face and shoved me backward. I was also dragged across the room by another man when I told him I was done with the relationship after finding drugs in his room (this same guy told me that I would never amount to anything more than a receptionist).
- And how could I forget about the dad I met at my daughter's school who swept me off my feet? The guy who, after we got engaged, convinced my dying grandfather—without me knowing—to "loan" him $80,000 (for reasons still unknown), and then decided to put the money in a secret bank account.

Needless to say, I ended things and called off the wedding. I had to send out cancellation notices to the 250 people on our guest list. It was mortifying. The shame and guilt I felt that my daughter had to go through this as well was overwhelming and beyond horrible. The only way I knew how to deal with the emotional pain was to numb it with alcohol.

- And last but not least, a few years later I met a guy through a mutual friend; this guy turned out to be the douche that sent me over the edge at the ripe age of thirty-five. He ended up being a pathological liar who lied about anything and everything—including the kind of sandwich he had for lunch—and the topper was when I figured out that he had lied about having cancer.

I wasn't kidding when I said toxic relationships—I couldn't make this stuff up. To be honest, I'm quite surprised I haven't been a guest on *Dateline*.

At this point, I felt like finding true love was a lost cause for me, and I was convinced I was destined to be a lonely old cat lady. I couldn't understand why I was attracting these types of relationships, and I just kept asking myself, "Why is this happening to me?!"

The problem was that after each relationship I found myself sinking further and further down into a dark hole filled with embarrassment, shame, guilt, blame, anger, resentment, and a shit ton of sadness. Even though I'd thought the rest of my life was good (outside of the men I was dating), in truth, I was at the lowest point of my life and silently suffering. I did my best to appear strong on the outside, but unfortunately there wasn't much room for weakness in my day-to-day life.

During the day, I was a senior executive assistant to top-level executives at a Fortune 500 company, and at night I was a single mother wearing multiple hats, doing my best to hold it together. There were many nights I climbed into bed feeling alone, broken, and helpless.

The emotional pain got worse and worse, and my frustration with my love life weighed on me more and more, but thankfully my motivation to change my life was absolutely crystal clear: my young daughter. I knew I was leading by example, and the example I was providing wasn't one I was proud of. The last thing I wanted was for *her* to wake up a hot mess like I was, or—God forbid—find herself in the same pattern of relationships I suffered through, thinking that *she* wasn't worthy of a man's love and respect.

I came home after that final breakup and looked at my daughter as she sat on her bed. I made myself a promise that I would do whatever work on myself I needed to do in order to be the best role model I could be for her.

I gave her life, but I believe she saved mine.

WHO THIS BOOK IS FOR

I wrote this book for women who have broken hearts, and who feel like they might never find a decent guy, even though they've tried. In the beginning, I meant for this book to be for women in their twenties, but in writing it, middle-aged women told me they couldn't wait to read this book too. You might be single and ready to mingle, in an "it's complicated" situation, divorced, or even in an unfulfilling relationship—no matter which category you fall into, you're likely wondering if there's a better way. There is. We'll look at how you can heal yourself to be a match for the relationship you truly desire and get you out of the rinse-and-repeat douchebag cycle.

HOW TO READ THIS BOOK

I'll tell you a lot of stories (unfortunately all true) about the men I dated who turned my world upside down, what they taught me, and what I wish I'd known. To protect their privacy, some names in this book are fictitious, and I indicate that by first using them with an asterisk (for example, Nick*).

As you read this book, take note of your feelings. I hope you laugh, and it's perfectly okay if you cry. Our emotions run deep, and sometimes hearing other women's stories can trigger the reopening of an old wound that needs to be healed, so I invite you to let the tears come and wash away the old pain that may be weighing heavily on your wounded heart.

My stories might make you think about a guy who broke your heart in the past, or maybe my stories will trigger memories of another hardship, one that isn't related to a romantic relationship. Hell, maybe my stories will frustrate you and you might find yourself judging me because you couldn't imagine ever dealing with the BS I put up with in my relationships—and that's okay too. I'm glad you haven't endured the heartaches that I have over the years. We are each on our own unique path, and we all have different messages to share with the world.

Whatever comes up for you as you read this book, pay attention to and honor your feelings and reactions. If you're being triggered, there's a good chance that there's a deeper wound, or a lesson to be learned. By doing this work you will create space for what you truly want in your life.

All the chapters end with a "Heal Yourself" section that provides self-guided journaling exercises to help you heal—and learn—from your past. Grab a journal so you can keep track of your progress and insights as you better understand yourself, whether you want to heal your past, set intentions for your future, or be present in the current moment. My intention is to help you discover a new way to see challenges in relationships, or realize why you may be stuck in a cycle of looking for love in all the wrong places, or in a cycle of being single.

Disclaimer: Some of the ideas I present in this book may be challenging for readers who have been severely traumatized in a relationship. I ask only that you work through this book with an open mind and see if you feel better after reading it.

Also, this book is not a substitute for mental health care or legal protection. Seek a mental health professional if you need to, or law enforcement and legal counsel if you are in an unsafe situation.

WE'RE IN THIS TOGETHER

My soul sisters helped me get through the darkest time of my life, and I'll be forever grateful for not only their friendship, but for helping me see the light when I couldn't do it on my own. Their love, support, and guidance meant (and means) the world to me.

Friendships are about being the love someone needs to pull themselves up in their darkest times or celebrate during their good times.

You may want to share what comes up for you while you read this book and need help to process your emotions, or would like dating support. For these reasons and more, I created a private community for readers to come together to share stories, connect, heal, and support one another. To gain access to this sisterhood or learn more about working with me directly, please go to www.staceydewald.com.

Okay—it's time to get to work so you can go from douchebags to diamonds, so buckle up, sister! It's a bumpy ride, but I promise you it's worth it. And if you're experiencing doubt about finding true love, please don't. If I can find love, so can you.

Thank you for joining me on this journey. I'm so glad you're here.

CHAPTER 1

The Prayer That Changed Everything

The last douchebag I dated lied to me about having cancer.

In the thick cloud of my anger, sadness, and frustration with myself for not seeing through his lies sooner, a voice that was louder than those feelings piped up and asked me, "What about my daughter?" I had to think of her and the kind of example I was setting when it came to relationships with men and what she could expect from them. If I kept getting lied to and used, what did that show her? (More about what happened with that toxic relationship in Chapter 5.)

That evening I started praying, HARD. I prayed for a miracle. I prayed for any form of help that would pull me out of the darkness. I prayed for the answers to help me understand how I got to this point in my life. I prayed for better days. I prayed for guidance to help me become a better mom. I was so desperate for change, and at that point I had no other choice than to trust that my prayers were being heard and help was on the way.

It wasn't long after that dark night of the soul that a good friend told me about a counselor who specialized in why people attract certain things and situations into their lives. And even though I had already gone to years of counseling and therapy, I immediately contacted him and scheduled a session.

In our first visit, I explained my string of heartbreaks and how I was pretty sure I was destined to be single for the rest of my life…until he stopped me mid-sentence and said, "Stacey, I hear you, but you're not a victim. Yes, you've been handed a few bad eggs, but maybe all of this happened to you for a reason…if you're open to seeing it that way."

What I *wanted* to say was, "Buddy, are you fucking kidding me right now?! A 'few' bad eggs? Did you NOT just hear what I told you? My ex-fiancé conned my dying grandfather out of $80,000, I had to call off a huge wedding and move out of my dream home, I'm positive I have liver failure at this point thanks to all the wine I've consumed, and the advice you give me is that maybe this happened for a reason?!"

But…I didn't. Something told me to keep my mouth shut and just listen.

"We can touch on your past, but I don't want to camp out there. I want to move you forward," he said.

"Um…you mean…there's hope for me?" I asked quietly.

"Yes," he replied with a gentle smile.

The best word to describe how I felt in that moment is…hope.

Hope that I wasn't broken.

Hope that I could be the mom I always wanted to be.

Hope that I'd be able to live a life that I could be proud of.

Hope that the emotional pain I was feeling was temporary.

"How?!" I eagerly asked.

It took him a minute to get his 6'8" body out of the biggest La-Z-Boy recliner I've ever seen, but once he got up, he walked to his bookshelf to grab a book.

"Here's your homework," he said. He handed me a copy of *Radical Forgiveness: A Revolutionary Five-Stage Process to Heal Relationships, Let Go of Anger and Blame, and Find Peace in Any Situation.*

"I think it will help you understand a bit more about what I'm talking about and how we can get you moving in the right direction."

I blinked at him. WTF? *Now I need to learn how to forgive these guys?! Okay, maybe coming here wasn't a good idea.* Even though I wasn't much of a reader, I was willing to try anything at that point, so I graciously took the book. That evening, I went home after work and, instead of focusing on which bottle of wine I was going to open, I focused on my homework. Within only a few pages, I was beginning to see that my counselor was an answer to my desperate prayers.

RADICAL FORGIVENESS

Radical Forgiveness by Colin Tipping changed my life. In his book, he highlights the difference between what we normally think of as "forgiveness," which keeps us in a victim mindset, and what he means by "radical forgiveness." His approach opens up space for us to look at painful events in our lives from a place of power instead of victimhood. His goal in writing the book is to help us make that shift. I wasn't so sure about the forgiveness part, but I was ready to stop being a victim to all these douchebags…if it was possible.

The story that grabbed me was Tipping's description of his sister's drama-filled marriage and what was going on underneath the surface. His sister, Jill, was obsessing about her husband's bad behavior toward her. I could totally relate. These men did all this awful stuff to us, so why shouldn't we think about it? Tipping offers a different viewpoint. What if, instead, there was something else going on besides them doing something to us? Something spiritual, divinely guided, and for her—or my—highest good.

In this light, moments when we are hurt give us an opportunity to heal an old wound instead of staying stuck in victimhood. Those old wounds will continue to cause us pain and impact our lives in different ways until we heal them. That's when we shift from being a victim to thinking, *Why is this happening for me?* as I discuss later in this book. For Tipping's sister, when he guides her to ask this question, the answer is startling. The wound wasn't really caused by her husband, it was caused years ago, when she was a little girl who didn't feel love from her father, and therefore felt unworthy of love. This sense of unworthiness remained in her subconscious as if it were an absolute truth, instead of just something she learned. Then, as an adult, when she bounced from one toxic relationship to the next, those men were treating her the way she expected to be treated, holding up a mirror that reflected how she felt about herself. In a way, those mirroring moments were the universe trying to tell her where she needed to heal. I could recognize myself in that example, and maybe you recognize yourself too.

This next part might be even more challenging. Now, these douchebags are holding up mirrors reflecting how we feel about ourselves, but in a way, the act of them showing us those mirrors isn't victimizing us—it's giving us a gift. The sooner we can recognize the gifts in those moments of hurt, the faster we can start healing old wounds or breaking down limiting beliefs, allowing us to instead be mirrors for healthier and more loving relationships.

Even though Jill's story wasn't exactly like mine, there was just something about her story that rocked me to my core. Little did I know how much my life was about to radically change, all thanks to a book I thought was going to be a waste of my time.

Another concept I learned from *Radical Forgiveness* is that whatever you believe about yourself to be true will influence how you see events and situations in your life. Those beliefs will cause you to find things in your life that support your viewpoint. If you think you're a victim, then you'll be able to name a list of times you were wronged. However, if you think you're a warrior, you'll refer back to all the times you survived tough situations. If you think you deserve compassion, you'll remember all the times you were shown compassion, and on it goes. For the first time, I wondered what limiting beliefs I was carrying, and what might be possible if I just believed that I belonged and was worthy of true love and respect. I was ready to find out.

DECIDING THE SHIT SHOW WAS OVER

From that evening on, I made a choice to start taking full responsibility for my life and showing up as my best self for my daughter. After reading one book and attending one therapy appointment, I wasn't suddenly 100% transformed, but at those times that I didn't live up to my new ideals, I would go back, clean up my mess, and take accountability for my behavior. Here are some changes I made:

- I immediately started focusing on what *was* working in my life versus what *wasn't,* and I vowed to allow zero space for any additional negativity or drama from others.
- I gave myself permission to be happy.
- Instead of spending my free time complaining about life with my friends, I used that time to learn anything and everything that I could get my hands on about the Law of Attraction. It was up to me to figure out what was going on in my inner world that was causing me to attract certain types of people and drama-filled situations to my outer world.
- I spent countless hours journaling about my behavior, thought patterns, habits, and limiting beliefs. Every single time I was emotionally triggered by someone or something, I would turn to my journal to reflect.

This self-reflection helped me shift my perspective. Instead of focusing on what others did to me, I focused on what it was in myself that had been open to that behavior or circumstance.

For example, a big part of taking responsibility for myself was to stop expecting (or creating) a shit show. Before doing this work, if I met a guy who didn't raise red flags, I'd always find things to be annoyed about and create some sort of drama, sabotaging the relationship and eventually pushing him away—or I would just break up with him. That was what felt normal to me, and in some twisted way it became my "normal" way of being. Deep down, I couldn't deal with having my heart broken or being rejected again, so I had to inflict the pain first and spend time trying to figure out what was wrong with the guy. What I should have been doing instead was spending that time trying to figure out what was wrong with *me*. So fucked up, I know, but this used to be my life prior to learning the tools I'm teaching you in this book.

I have done every activity that I teach you in the "Heal Yourself" sections at the end of each chapter. From experience, I know that some exercises will be easier than others, but they're all necessary if you want to do the healing work and find the gift hidden in the bad relationships of your past and stop attracting douchebags. The healing process starts with understanding yourself and your emotions so you can work with them to evolve and be a match for loving relationships. I learned a lot from all that self-reflection—here are some of the high points:

- The universe was aligning me with people, things, and situations that matched the energy I was putting out—I didn't feel worthy of love and respect, so therefore I attracted many men who mirrored this belief. (If you're struggling with being single at any age, you too may have a deep belief that you aren't worthy of love, and so therefore you don't attract any men at all.)
- I would be loved and respected only as much as I loved and respected myself.
- I needed to be open-minded and willing to see things differently in my relationships if I wanted to break the cycle of attracting unhealthy relationships and see lasting change.
- There was wisdom in my wounds (don't get me wrong—these guys were absolute douchebags, but today I'm grateful for each of those men because they showed me what I needed to heal within myself so that I could become the woman that I am today).
- If I couldn't learn how to see obstacles in relationships as opportunities for personal growth—no matter how

dysfunctional it may seem—I would continue to make life harder than it really had to be, staying stuck in the cycle of unwanted situations and attracting the wrong people, and I would never live a life that I truly desired.

What happened after I gained all this clarity was nothing short of a miracle.

I'll tell you the whole love story in Chapters 10 and 11, but essentially, less than four months after adopting this new way of being, I attracted a handsome, kind-hearted, funny, honest, successful, and loyal man who eventually became my husband in 2013. The transformation that I experienced was so powerful that it inspired me to become a Certified Life Coach in 2015, and a Certified Reiki Practitioner in 2018.

I'm an advocate of personal development and emotional healing, and I believe that emotional triggers are opportunities for personal growth—especially when it comes to relationships. I live and breathe the same principles that I teach my clients and my own child. I am a firm believer that anybody can change their life if they are open to examining their behavior, emotional triggers, and struggles on a deep soul level, and are willing to shift their mindset from "Why is this happening *to* me?" to "Why is this happening *for* me?" I invite you to do the same, starting with this first "Heal Yourself" exercise.

Heal Yourself
DEALING WITH HEARTACHE

Great news! You have options for how to deal with your heartache. You can sit on the porch and drink yourself into oblivion like I did, or you can help the healing process by doing one of the following:

- When it comes to healing a heartache that leaves you feeling horrible, I have good news. There's a shortcut. I only wish I'd known about tapping, also known as the Emotional

Freedom Technique (or EFT), years ago. I could have dealt with processing my emotions, evaluating my deep-rooted beliefs, and healing my heartache a lot sooner.

EFT has been proven to rewire the brain to put the unconscious "blocks" that keep us stuck and unable to move forward in our lives into the metaphorical trash can—for good. This rewiring helps us shift our unconscious beliefs and emotions.

By tapping on your meridian points while processing emotions and thoughts, you don't just feel better from the endorphins, but you also release what's causing the stress. FYI, tapping can also work for physical pain, grief, addiction, weight loss, insomnia, shame, guilt, financial stress, and a variety of other things. I use the Tapping Solution app multiple times a day to release overwhelm, overthinking, anxiety, fear, and procrastination, or if I need a quick attitude adjustment. To learn more about how EFT works, visit www.thetappingsolution.com.

- Try breathwork, which is a great way to clear low-vibe energy that may be stuck in your body. Our bodies go through a lot during/following a loss, so when you feel these uncomfortable feelings, sit with them and send them love. Put one hand on your stomach and the other on your heart and imagine breathing love in through your nose and breathing pain out through your mouth. Repeat the breathing pattern until you feel better. I suggest finding a certified breathwork facilitator like my friend, Vaughn Pierro. You can find out more about her at www.vaughnpierro.com.

- Write down all the reasons why you broke up so that when you miss him, you can pull the letter out and remind yourself why things ended and why you are better off without him. This will help keep your ego in check when it tries to convince you that you're lonely and tells you that contacting him is a good idea (it's not). Remember, there's an "X" in front of his name for a reason.

- Take a bath with one cup of Epsom salts. The salt helps ground your energy and is a great detoxifier for negative energy and heavy emotions. Before you get into the bath, set an intention for what you want to let go of and what you want to bring in.
- Write your feelings out so you're not holding them inside. Journal about your emotions and what happened. If you went through a breakup and feel you didn't get the closure you deserve, write a letter to your ex, then shred it, burn it, or flush it down the toilet—but whatever you do, do not send it.
- Stop following him on social media, stop asking his friends or family about him, and for the love of God, do not contact him and beg him to take you back. You're better than that.
- Give yourself space from your ex's family and mutual friends until you have had more time to process the breakup.
- Take note of if you ask yourself questions such as "What did I do wrong? Why am I not good enough for him?" "How could he just walk away and not love me anymore?" or "How can he like her more than me?" These are all questions I asked myself in the past, but what if I told you that he just did you a huge favor and someone better is on the way? I wish someone had told me that back in the day. It would have saved a lot of tears and anguish.

Feeling is healing. Take the time to heal your heart through the grieving process and allow the tears to flow.

CHAPTER 2

What the Mindfuck?

I once dated a pizza delivery guy.

This was when I was much younger, so maybe that doesn't sound so bad, but Evan* was older than me. My family wasn't fond of him, and that made me really dig my heels in when it came to the relationship. It wasn't just that he delivered pizzas, but he came from the wrong end of town.

However, it wasn't just poverty that I tried to save him from. I felt like I needed to save him because he had a drinking problem. A lot of the time Evan was fun when he was drinking, and I would think he could handle himself. Then, at other times, I wouldn't be able to get ahold of him because he was passed out. One time I even took him to the hospital because he had alcohol poisoning. Each time, he assured me it would never happen again, and that he would change.

I believed him, every time.

Evan and I developed a codependent pattern of him needing help or love or care, and me rushing in to provide. Then, he would do something mean, blame me for his bad attitude, and apologize profusely after he sobered up. That situation has a name: a mindfuck.

MIND·FUCK

/ˈmīndˌfək/

VULGAR SLANG

noun

A disturbing or extremely confusing experience, in particular one that is caused by deliberate psychological manipulation.

You might have also heard this called "gaslighting," which is what happened when I'd see Evan do something rude, or even spiteful, and call him out, only to have him turn the tables on me and make me feel like a jerk for even bringing it up. Over time, this became a sort of mind control. It caused me to constantly second-guess myself, so eventually I just stayed quiet.

I see now that I was projecting what I wanted, which was someone to take care of me, but that was never going to happen because I was an empath, and Evan was an alcoholic narcissist. Empaths are highly sensitive people whose emotions can be affected by the people around them, even if they aren't aware it's happening. If you recognize yourself as being an empath, it's crucial to protect your energy, especially from narcissists like Evan. Narcissism is a personality disorder, the hallmark of which involves someone thinking the world revolves around them, and they can do no wrong. So, they don't take criticism well and will gaslight and manipulate those around them all day and night to get what they want. For an empath that's presuming their goodwill, this is a toxic combination. (If you're wondering if you might be an empath, *The Empath's Survival Guide* by Judith Orloff, MD, helped me understand that part of myself.)

This was a dysfunctional mindfuck of a relationship that unfortunately lasted many years. Instead of thinking "Do I want to invest myself here?" or considering my own boundaries, safety, or happiness, I was all about taking care of Evan.

That relationship finally ended on a camping trip with a few of his buddies.

We were camped in the middle of a field, and it was late. We were already in our sleeping bags, and his friends tapped on the tent to invite him to drink by the river. Without a glance in my direction, he unzipped the tent to head out. I sat up.

"Please don't go. I'm tired," I said.

"So go to sleep," he muttered.

"You're not leaving me here alone in the middle of nowhere."

Suddenly his hand shoved my face backward, and my head hit the ground. I didn't understand why he would do this to someone he cared about...*oh*. He did me a favor when he turned around and went toward the river, leaving me crying and holding the side of my face. In that moment I knew I was done.

I had some other early relationships with guys who had less than I did. My interest came from wanting to give those men things they didn't have and make them feel special (secretly hoping they would return the favor and make me feel special). But, in the end, all that stuff I bought for them wasn't enough for them to respect me and love me. I even had another ex-boyfriend tell me I'd never amount to anything more than a receptionist, and then he dragged me across the floor to prove his point: that *he* was in control. That's when I finally broke up with him for good, but why did I have to get pushed that far to decide to leave? It was mind games.

Ever had a guy mess with your head? The mindfuck goes something like this: He is on his best behavior for the first couple of months, he tells you everything you want to hear, and he does everything you want him to do. He builds you up...only to slowly tear you down and eventually make you second-guess your self-worth. You start to feel insecure and you stop listening to your gut, which is telling you to get the hell out of the relationship, NOW! You may respond with "But the sex is so good I can't leave," or "I can't break up with him—he has the best family!" or "We've been together for so long, I don't want to start over in another relationship," or "It's not *that* bad," or "We have kids together," or any other excuse you can come up with to avoid feeling the pain of a breakup or being single again…until one day you wake up asking yourself "How in the *hell* did I end up here?!" I get it. I've been there, done that, and got a couple of t-shirts.

THE SERIAL CHEATER

A girlfriend once told me, "If you spend as much time on your inside as you do your outside, you may just meet a nice guy." Thank you? Looking back, she was 100% correct, but unfortunately, I didn't listen and attracted another douchebag.

This douche was Nick*. Not only was he charismatic and extremely fit, but he was also a wealthy business-owner. Surely an entrepreneur would know how to treat a young lady, right? By then, I was in my mid-twenties, and my daughter, Jaide, was a toddler. He was in his early thirties. I thought that meant he was stable.

The chemistry between Nick and I was off the charts, so I was really surprised when a mutual friend said to me, "I can't believe you're dating Nick." I asked him why he would say that, and he said Nick was a total player and I was going to get hurt. *Well*, I thought, *that might've been true in the past, but we have such a connection, there's no way he would do that to me.* Wishful thinking.

The first time I knew something was wrong was when a girl called my home on a Saturday morning, asking if Nick was with me.

"No," I replied, "He left a little while ago…but who is this? And why do you want to know if he's here?"

It turned out this girl was looking for him because they were dating, and he ghosted her the night prior. I say "girl" because she was only nineteen years old, in a full-on relationship with my boyfriend—who was in the process of buying her a new car. *Good to know.*

As Maya Angelou once said, "When someone shows you who they are, believe them the first time." Many times, my inner voice piped up about warning signs I noticed with Nick, and so many other guys I dated when they showed me their true colors—but I ignored that voice. I would see behavior that bothered me and think, *Excuse me?!*

But I didn't say anything, and I didn't do anything about it, partly because I didn't want to deal with it, but also because I honestly didn't fully understand what I was dealing with—one day Nick was nice to me, and the next he would make me feel like a horrible person. Classic gaslighting. And I was totally susceptible to it.

Let him show you who he really is and what he's about, so wait at least six months before making any hasty decisions. Trust me, if he's shaming you or trying to control you in the courting stage of dating, I promise you it will only get worse from there. If you recognize some of the qualities I've mentioned in your own partner, you're probably dating a narcissist and in a cycle of gaslighting. Ask yourself—is he making you feel horrible if you speak up about HIS bad behavior? You deserve better. But there's hope. I learned years later that when you're in control of your emotions and not susceptible to manipulation, that is like a mindfuck repellent, because these guys love to play on your emotions to try to dim your light. However, they can't play with your emotions or gaslight you if you see them coming a mile away. Keep reading, and I'll give you all the signs to look out for at the end of this chapter.

But back to Nick—it blew my mind that a guy could have such a deep connection with me while simultaneously having a full-on relationship with another woman. *What the mindfuck?!* What was wrong with me that caused him to find someone else? That's what my younger self thought.

I decided to confront him, and boy did I. I knew where he was, so the girl and I headed that way. You should have seen the look on his face when both of us showed up. He bolted out the back door and I ran out the front to see him trying to drive away. Pure rage flooded my body, and my only goal was to get in his truck and break his nose (classy, I know). I did manage to get into his truck, but his large biceps intercepted my flailing arms, blocking his face. Meanwhile, the young gal stood on the sidewalk in complete shock. This was not one of my proudest moments. It was bad. *Really* bad.

See, Nick told me he loved me and only me, and I believed him. I figured if I believed him, then the emotional pain would magically go away…but of course it didn't. As a young woman, I internalized my emotions and convinced myself it had to be me that was the problem—*I must not be good enough for him*, I thought (especially because this other girl was six years younger than me). I started blaming myself, when I should have been blaming him for being an asshole.

The cheating didn't stop. Every time I caught him and confronted him, he would ramp up the head games and gaslighting. The more he gaslighted me, the more I felt like I was going crazy. The more I felt like I was going crazy, the more I was spiraling out of control—as was he. The more I tried to manipulate him or our situation in some fucked-up, unhealthy way, the more I found myself in the "break up and make up" cycle. He would break up with me, seemingly every Friday, and then "miss me" again on Monday. Go figure. This worked great for him—he could do whatever he wanted over the weekend and not have to answer to me or explain anything, because we weren't technically together. I dreaded the weekends.

This was the ultimate mindfuck.

In true narcissistic fashion, to deflect from his own behavior, he would turn the tables and put the attention on me, accusing *me* of cheating on him. He used my innocence against me, to control me, so I had to check in with him all the time to prove to him that I wasn't cheating. He was in a cycle of cheating, begging forgiveness, and making up, and every time, the stakes got higher. I took on his behavior and drove myself crazy, wondering *What did I do wrong? Why does it have to be like this?*

Even my family tried to get involved. I remember my dad saying, "Shorty, I can't believe you're still dealing with this guy. It's like you keep hitting your thumb with a hammer. At what point do you just move your thumb?" It was an interesting analogy, and he had a valid point. What was it going to take for me to walk away from this guy? Why didn't I love and respect myself enough to walk away from such a dysfunctional relationship? Why did I feel this was the best I could do? Unfortunately, my dad didn't know about the threats I was receiving from Nick, my true mental state in the relationship, or the web of mindfuckery I was tangled in.

Things continued to escalate. Nick was positive that I had something going on with one of my guy friends. He was adamant that men and women can't be just friends, and that men only wanted in my pants. He made comments about who I was talking to and when. There was nothing going on with any of these friends of mine, but how did he know (A) who I was talking to, and (B) when? I listened to my gut and contacted my cell phone company to see if there was any way he could access my account. The customer service rep asked to confirm both addresses listed on the account.

"Both addresses?" I questioned.

"Yes, it looks like a gentleman called in a few months ago and requested that your statements be sent to an additional address than what's on file."

"And you allowed this?" *I was not happy.* I immediately got Nick's address deleted and secured my account with a password. This was only the beginning.

The situation worsened, and soon Nick was calling me at my office up to twenty-five times a day. I would just let the calls go to voicemail because I had work to do. He would leave messages like "I can't live without you," or "You're going to regret not answering my call," or the one that put chills down my spine: "You're going to find my dead body on your porch when you get home from work if you don't call me back!" As hard as it was, I would ignore his calls all day, but it only made him more upset. Eventually, he went to the extent of test-driving a car just so that he could wait for me in my office building's parking garage without me knowing he was there. He knew that if I saw his truck, I wouldn't walk to my car.

One day, I took the elevator down to the garage level, like I do every day. The elevator door slid open, and I didn't see Nick's truck, so I continued to my car. Suddenly, he jumped out of a random car and ran toward me, yelling, "Stacey! Please talk to me. I love you! Why won't you pick up my calls?!"

At the time, I thought *Wow, this guy must really love me to go through all this effort.* However, knowing what I know now, I recognize that he never had any intention of killing himself for me. It was just another tactic to control me with a good old-fashioned mindfuck.

After two years of dealing with Nick, I was completely brainwashed, to the point that I believed him and felt that these messages proved that he truly loved me, although I didn't know what to do with that kind of "love."

In a later chapter I'll tell you how this mess ended, but right now I want to say that for me, this guy was like a drug. My friends would say I was *dickmitized*, because no matter how bad things got, I couldn't stay away from him. Toward the end, I started becoming aware that I was in a pattern of addiction and would think, *Why can't I let this guy go?* Even after things finally ended, I was afraid to run into him. It was like avoiding a drug dealer.

The control Nick had over me fed my confusion over why he would repeatedly cheat on me, but then use "I love you" as a way to keep me in the relationship. As long as he could keep me feeling insecure, I remained trapped in a dysfunctional relationship. The more I gave Nick that authority over my wellbeing, the harder it was to get out.

The old me would have really benefited from stopping to think:

Why is this happening for me?

Instead, I kept asking myself:

What's wrong with me?

Why am I so broken and fucked up?

Why am I so weak?

Why don't I love myself enough to leave him?

What I didn't understand then was that the change I desperately wanted needed to start with me. I couldn't change how this guy was treating me, but I could have changed what I was tolerating. I deserved respect, but first I had to truly believe it and learn how to respect myself.

As women, and especially as female empaths, I find that we tend to blame ourselves, or think we did something wrong when a man steps out on a relationship or refuses to fully commit to us. The only thing we're doing wrong is allowing the behavior to continue. If he chooses to cheat (whether emotionally or physically) or has an issue fully committing to you, you get to choose whether or not he gets to play in your sandbox, not him.

I believe the whole mess with Nick could have been avoided if I only knew then what I know now about resisting mindfucks and how to spot a narcissist, but apparently I had to go through it so I could one day write a book in the hopes of helping women like yourself dodge the bullets that I took to the chest. We are each on our own journey, and I wish I had a magic spell that would prevent you from ever being heartbroken again, or meeting a douchey guy, but I don't. Instead, what I can do is share my story and hope that it guides you in the opposite direction of heartbreak; the direction toward wholeheartedly loving yourself and feeling confident AF about what you deserve and what you will not tolerate for one more second of your precious life. I want you to know, without a shadow of a doubt, that you are worthy of being loved and treated with respect.

Don't accept anything less than treatment worthy of a queen. What you allow will continue.

Heal Yourself
FOUR WAYS TO HACK INTO YOUR EMOTIONS

I told you earlier that when you're aware of your feelings, you can more easily recognize how others might be trying to manipulate your feelings. These four exercises will help you listen to your feelings and learn to tell the difference between those true messages from your heart and the untruths that someone else could be trying to make you believe.

1. Emotions are always a gauge of where we're at internally, so let's see what's really going on with your feelings now.
The sooner you acknowledge your feelings, the sooner you will detach from the pain and heal, instead of being trapped in a dead-end relationship. That's why it's important to understand our emotions and

know where we're at with them at any given moment. I had low self-esteem, even as a successful woman, because I still looked to men to fill the void that I felt within myself. Below, I share some questions you can ask yourself to work through your emotions and how they might have influenced your relationships. Consider your present relationship that isn't bringing you happiness and reflect on these questions:

- Is this all you think you deserve? If so, why? Who told you that this is all you deserve?
- Can you tell me three things you love about the person who is causing you so much pain?
- What is making you stay in this relationship?
- What are you getting out of this relationship?
- Would you be happier if you left this relationship?
- Do you feel you are compromising equally, or is it an unbalanced give and take?
- Are you holding on to this relationship because you're afraid of being alone? If so, why? What is it about being alone that scares you?
- Do you struggle with abandonment issues? Where did this originate? What forgiveness work needs to be done here? If so, who is it that you need to forgive?

If you were to rate your level of self-love, what would that number be on a scale of one (nada) to ten (totally obsessed with loving myself)?

2. Use your emotions as your own personal spiritual guide.

Notice what emotions you tend to experience in your relationships (sadness or joy, fulfillment or emptiness, anger or happiness, love or rejection) and use them to guide you in this healing process. For example, if I feel irritated, I allow myself to feel irritated, but whether it lasts one day or two weeks, I eventually will spend time asking my emotions, *What's up with all this irritation?* Give this technique a try the next time someone emotionally triggers you, or you reflect on a painful relationship from the past, and go through the exercise now:

Close your eyes (this will help calm your overactive mind).

Put one hand on your heart and the other one on your stomach, over your belly button.

Inhale slowly through your nose and exhale out through your mouth.

Grab your journal and ask yourself the following questions (close your eyes after each question if you really want to go deeper and hear the truth):

- What is *really* bothering me about this situation?
- When have I felt like this before?
- What does this situation remind me of?
- How did *I* show up in the situation?
- Could I have shown up as a better version of myself? If so, how?
- Why is this happening for me?

I take the time to do this because I know that if I don't bring what is *really* going on underneath the trigger up to the surface, then the trend of irritation will continue and I will attract more situations or people to be irritated about. The best part is, you get to choose. Personally, I've made a commitment to myself to do this work every time I'm triggered in my relationships because I've seen the incredible benefits of this work and how quickly things shift once I'm able to see the purpose in the pain.

3. Understand your emotional wounds so douchebags can't mess with your head.

Mindfucks happen when douchebags zero in on your emotional triggers and past pain. When you know what yours are, they can't be used against you so easily.

Consider your past relationships that didn't bring you happiness and go through the questions as many times as necessary to cover all the relationships.

Write your answers in your journal:

- What do you need to let go of from this past relationship that is no longer serving you?
- What beliefs are you still carrying from this relationship?
- What emotions still come up when you think about this relationship?

As you reflect on your answers to these questions, some patterns may emerge. You may be realizing more about your relationships. Choose a couple of these realizations and write your declarations for what emotions or patterns you're letting go of below:

Declare what you are letting go of (for example, you may realize you're angry about how you were treated): _____

_____

Declare what you are bringing into your life instead (for example, if codependency is something you want to let go of, then you would bring in learning how to have trust in yourself and improve your self-esteem): _____

For example: "I'm letting go of anger and bringing into my life abundance, joy, happiness, love, kindness, and forgiveness."

If these emotions don't have an outlet to be released, you will attract the same level and quality of emotion and pain in your next relationship—or even worse, another douchebag. This is why it's so important to heal our inner world before jumping into another relationship, and why I suggest not getting involved with a man who is fresh out of a breakup. That situation never ends well, at least in my experience.

4. Pick up the puppy (this is a great tool if you have a hard time working through your emotions).

What would you do if the cutest little puppy whimpered at your feet? Would you ignore it, or would you pick it up and comfort it? Of course you would pick it up! Well, imagine that your emotions need to be comforted, just like that little puppy. How do you think you would feel if you gave your emotions the same love and attention? I'll give you a clue: You'd feel amazing!

By the way, it's important to remember that these uncomfortable emotions won't go away until you deal with them (more about that in a later chapter).

CLASSIC GASLIGHTING PHRASES

Listen for these common manipulation phrases that could be signs that you're with a narcissist who's using gaslighting to play with your mind and keep you under their control. When you call them out, they'll deflect and say things like:

- This is all in your head.
- I didn't say that.
- You misunderstood me.
- That didn't happen.
- You're just remembering what you want to.

At other times, they'll control and change the conversation to put you in a position where you feel you need to comfort them, even though you're the one who is hurt:

- I'm so worthless. I don't know why you're with me.
- I love you so much, you know I would never hurt you on purpose—don't you?

- You deserve someone better.
- I'm such a loser.

Lastly, they'll make it your fault that you even brought up their behavior, usually by saying something like this:

- Why are you so sensitive?
- You take things too personally.
- Calm down. You're hysterical.
- You're crazy.
- Your friends and family don't even like you.

Start with awareness. When you can look at how someone hurt you and call it what it was, you regain some power and control over yourself, your feelings, and your truth. Seek help from a professional if you feel you are struggling to get out of a relationship with a narcissist. If you're seeking a divorce from a narcissist, I recommend contacting attorney Rebecca Zung, who specializes in these cases.

In the next chapter, you'll see that these narcissistic guys aren't necessarily all violent or cheaters—you might be with a narcissist even if he's not an obvious douchebag, and those guys are harder to spot. I should know—I almost married one.

CHAPTER 3

Dicks with Benefits

I was chatting recently with some young women about a cute guy one of them was dating. It turned out that he worked for the NFL. The girls were asking, "Can he get you tickets to the games?"

"Yes!" one of the girls squealed with excitement. "OMG, he's a dick with benefits!"

"Whoa, I have to know," I said. "What's a dick with benefits?"

"That's a guy who takes you on nice trips, or buys you expensive things, or in this case, can get tickets to NFL games and concerts," one of them explained.

"So basically, a dick with benefits is about how you benefit from his wealth and status?" I asked.

"Yep!"

I didn't want to go all motherly on them, or encourage them to ditch the dicks with benefits, but a million thoughts crossed my mind about the dicks with benefits *I* dated, and how each one went over like a fart in church. For one, think about Nick, who bought me a new BMW, but who was also a totally insane cheater. But he wasn't even close to being the most disastrous dick with benefits I ever dated.

No, that honor goes to a guy named Todd*. I should've seen it coming when I first met him for drinks at El Gaucho. I admit, I was impressed by the stylish restaurant he'd suggested. He was at the bar, drinking a dirty martini and reading *Yachts International*. When I walked up, he put the magazine down and said in a Rico Suavé voice, "Hello there." *What a douche*, I thought, but I sat down and ordered a drink anyway. Every fiber of my being was telling me to get out of there, but he was handsome, he had a daughter in Jaide's class, and I heard through the moms at school that he was a very successful businessman.

After a couple of cocktails and great conversation, he dropped what should've been a bomb. "Just so you know...I'm living with my ex-fiancée and her children at the moment, but I'm looking for a new place," he said. He said it so casually, like he was asking me to pass him the Grey Poupon.

"Oookay...I appreciate your honesty, but I'm really not interested in hanging out with someone living with their ex and her kids. Thanks for the drinks," I said. I picked up my purse and walked out, wondering, *How the fuck do I keep meeting these guys who have all this baggage and aren't fully available?*

I figured out later why I was a douche magnet and attracting emotionally unavailable men. Energetically, that was happening because I was emotionally unavailable, just like them. Love was scary and didn't feel safe, so I would unconsciously attract men who didn't want to be tied down and were only interested in one thing. Don't get me wrong, that setup is fine—as long as both parties received the memo that it is indeed only about sex, because ladies, just because you do the horizontal dance with a guy does not mean you're exclusively dating. Read that again.

This may sound harsh, but if you just want a guy based on the size of his wallet, then my guess is you're probably not interested in a truly meaningful relationship. I know this firsthand because that used to be me after I ditched the pizza delivery guy. It's like a guy who just wants a beautiful woman on his arm because of what he can gain from her status and beauty—ew. It's gross when guys do it, and it rarely works out for us, either.

Anyway, back to Todd. That night should've been our only date, but it wasn't.

GETTING SUCKED IN

The first time I saw Todd, I was dropping Jaide off at school. He was a handsome, well-dressed guy with an adorable little girl. My daughter caught me looking and said, "That's Isabelle's* dad. He volunteers in our class every week. He has really pretty eyes."

I wasn't looking for a relationship at that point, so I was just window-shopping the man candy, but I liked the sound of a volunteer dad. I thought it sounded way more stable and family-oriented than the other douches I'd dated. A few weeks later, I was on a work trip and checked in with Jaide, who was staying with her grandparents.

"Mommy, I've got good news!" she said.

"What is it, sweetie?" I asked. I thought it must be a new friend or a good grade on a test.

"Isabelle's dad gave me his number for you!"

It turned out that Todd had approached my daughter in the classroom and given her his number. Mind you, she was in elementary school, so it was a really big deal that Isabelle's cute dad wanted to go on a date with her mom. I didn't want to come across as desperate, so I waited a few days to reach out, and we made plans to meet after work at El Gaucho.

You know how that date went, but the next day he called me and asked me to meet him downstairs at my office. He was parked in front of the building in his black Jaguar. The driver's side window lowered. "Hop in," he said with a smirk.

"Umm, okay." I got into the car with him (had I not watched enough murder shows to know this was NOT a good idea?!). Then I noticed the backseat, which was full of clothes and random stuff.

"What's all this?"

"I moved out. I'm all yours." *Shut the front door.* Ladies, if a man makes a major life change after you refuse to date him, just so you know—you don't owe him anything. I wish I knew this back then.

I felt stuck, like someone was suffocating me. *You're not moving in with me,* I thought. I really like my own space.

"All mine, huh?" Instead of paying attention to the red flags, I ignored them and felt like I owed it to him to give "us" a chance. Even though he might actually have moved in with us if I allowed it, I didn't. He soon found a place to live.

The next week, he told me, "I love you." Yes, after one week of dating.

My inner voice was saying, *WTF, you barely know me,* but I chalked his comment up to something said in the heat of the moment.

Nope. He continued saying he loved me, so I thought, *Okay, I guess I'm in a relationship now.* When I look back and think how I felt right then, I was flattered that he was head over heels for me, but I wasn't stopping to check in with myself about what I thought about him. He wanted to get involved with Jaide right away, and her birthday party was where he made that move, offering to help me throw it for her. I didn't need his help, but I let him come over, and he made a point to show the other dads dropping their kids off that he was staying, and we were a couple.

He felt like a Disneyland dad. You know, the kind that tries to be the "fun dad," instead of doing what's best for the kids. He gave his daughter and Jaide gifts to win them over. However, to be honest, that wasn't too far from how I was parenting at the time either, out of guilt over where I had fallen short. I was trying to give my daughter the stuff I hadn't been able to give her before.

Giving Jaide things she wanted hit a critical point when Todd started sending me listings of homes for sale in the expensive part of town, asking me which ones I liked. I thought we were playing a fun game of "Let's imagine living in these mansions," so I responded to his email with my favorite. It was a stunning $1,100,000 home—quite different from the condo my daughter and I lived in. The house had a big bonus room, walk-in closets, and a big backyard for a dog. What if Todd could make that happen for us? Talk about a dick with benefits.

I settled into the new relationship, thankful that at least he wasn't cheating on me, stalking me, or calling twenty-five times a day. In that mindset, I was just noticing the lowest common denominator, that he wasn't being an asshole. I've watched this over the years with my girl-friends, too. When a guy isn't cheating, lying, manipulative, or drunk, they stay, even though they're not actually happy or in love. Settling should never be an option.

DISNEYLAND BOYFRIEND

Two months into the relationship, we went for a drive after going to a nice dinner. Suddenly, Todd pulled into a random driveway. It took a second for me to register that the driveway belonged to the house I'd sent him a link to. "What are we doing here?" I asked.

He handed me a greeting card that said, "Welcome home, baby," and a house key fell out.

I couldn't wait to tell Jaide. No part of me considered whether I wanted to live with him or not. We got busy furnishing the place, and he probably spent close to $50,000. At the time, that was about what I made in a year at my corporate job, and I was super impressed with the new lifestyle I had fallen into. Todd said the expensive new furnishings were needed because he didn't have much to bring into the house, since his ex got the furniture. I didn't question the logic there, but in hindsight, it's more likely that he moved in with just what was in his car and then left the same way.

A month later, we were having lunch at a beautiful country club, and he surprised me with a gorgeous two carat diamond ring. At that point, we weren't actually living together because I wasn't about to move out of my condo until I knew he was in it for the long haul. The ring showed me he was committed to our future together. We moved in together, although I didn't put my condo on the market. As we planned our future, he told me I didn't have to work, and he would support my daughter and me. I quit my corporate job to be a stay-at-home mom, which thrilled Jaide—she didn't have to go to before- and after-school daycare, and I was happy to spend more time with her.

Living with Todd was over the top. At night, he laid out my toothbrush with toothpaste on it. He would also replace my razor blades for me in the shower. The master bathroom had a double shower head, so I would often turn around to find him hopping in the shower with me. *OMG, I miss living alone,* I thought. I wondered if this was just what it was like to be married, but truthfully, I found all the attention a bit much. It was a total mindfuck for a guy to do things like that because it made me think, *Wow, he must really love me,* so I felt like I couldn't tell him to give me some elbow room in the shower, to stop touching my razor, or for fuck's sake, stop touching my toothbrush.

Todd spoiled us with shopping sprees, beautiful jewelry, and a first-class trip to Maui, where we stayed at the luxury Grand Wailea Maui Resort. He even let us get a new puppy that Jaide decided to name Max.

By then, he'd hired a high-end wedding planner to coordinate our big dream wedding, which was scheduled for that fall at the beautiful country club where he had proposed.

You'd think the pampering, vacations, and shopping sprees would be enough to keep our chemistry booming, but it was the complete opposite. We had been together for not even a year, and we were already having issues. Of course I blamed myself: *Does he not find me attractive? Why won't he touch me? OMG—he thinks I'm fat.* He blamed work stress, but my friend said it was "guilt dick." Supposedly, she explained, when a guy has a big secret, sometimes it affects their plumbing. I didn't see how that could be the issue though, because what terrible secret could this guy have? He barely ever left the house. He wasn't cheating—was he?

We even had a joint checking account to pay the household bills. I did the banking in our relationship because I'm a control freak when it comes to my finances, but maybe my gut told me to watch our account closely. We had an $8,500 house payment coming up and there was barely enough in the account to cover it. So, I asked him when he was going to receive his bonus.

He snapped, "Don't worry about it. I'll get the money."

"Actually, I am going to worry about it because our bank account is close to zilch—"

At that point, he stormed out. I sat there at the table, thinking *(A) don't be a dick, and (B) what do you mean don't worry about it?!*

Soon after the big engagement party at our new house, his behavior started to change even more. He wasn't his usual do-everything-for-Stacey-to-make-sure-she's-happy self. I kept asking him what was wrong, and he kept telling me that he was just stressed at work, waiting for clients to pay him.

Something didn't feel right.

But this was only the beginning...

Heal Yourself
FIND THE RED FLAGS

Every time something didn't feel right and I questioned it, or wanted to, I would just end up accepting Todd's answers, or I'd tell myself I was wrong. Basically, he was gaslighting me. Not trusting my intuition got me deeper and deeper into a relationship that—spoiler alert—didn't end well. What was happening was I would doubt myself when I saw a red flag because of all these limiting beliefs in my head. Like, *Who am I to question this guy?* Or, *Maybe I'm just so broken, I can't recognize a good guy when I have one.* Or, *Is this all in my head?*

Reflect on any troubling moments that you chose to ignore in your past relationships, or focus on one relationship in particular that's bothering you now. Write your answers to the following questions in your journal:

- What were the red flags?
- Have you seen these red flags in other relationships?

- How did it feel when you didn't listen to your gut telling you that something was off?
- Why did you choose to ignore them?
- Do you feel like you settled, or wasted time in a relationship due to not listening to your gut?
- What do you wish you'd done differently?

The point of this exercise is not to beat yourself up over the past, but rather to understand it so that you can make different choices going forward the next time you see a red flag, and have happier relationships as a result.

CHAPTER 4

Happily Never After

Remember that I had kept my condo when Jaide and I moved in with Todd? My grandpa was one major reason for that—he helped me buy it when Jaide was a baby. At the time, she was only a few months old, and I was just twenty-two years old, living with my parents after things went south with my daughter's dad.

I appreciated my parents' support, but my grandpa knew it was time for us to move. It was kind of him to notice that we needed our own space, and I couldn't afford a place on my own making $7.25 an hour as a receptionist at a law firm. This financial assistance was something he was able to do for us because he'd made his fortune in commercial real estate, but you would never know he was wealthy to look at him. He always wore a light blue, freshly pressed, short-sleeve button-up shirt, whether he was working in the yard or attending a meeting with his attorney—in which case he would then dress it up with his favorite dark blue Members Only jacket. He drove tasteful, but not flashy, cars, and didn't have a huge, gaudy watch like the men I met who were all flash and no cash. He was happy with the free watch he got from his bank. He was also very generous, and gave extensions to his renters who were ill and unable to work.

Now that I was getting married to Todd and didn't need my condo, the plan was to sell it. My grandfather had paid for new carpet and fresh painting for the interior, since when it sold, he'd get that investment back and then some.

It was bittersweet to think about selling the condo because it was a connection to my grandpa, who I was always very close to. When I was a little girl, I spent a lot of time with him and my grandma at their beach house in Tulalip, Washington. When I was there (and not busy dressing up in my grandma's high heels to wear around the house) my grandpa and I would do things together, like digging up clams. We'd pull crab pots and walk the beach so I could collect colorful starfish and stack them on my arm (I would then return them to the water after our short walk—don't worry, no starfish were hurt).

After I moved in with Todd, sometimes I'd go for a drive from my new house and wind up sitting on my condo's porch. It didn't make sense to me that I was feeling pulled back there when I lived in my dream house, with everything Jaide and I could ever want. And yet, I felt more at home at my old place.

INTENTIONS REVEALED

By July, it was time to mail the 250 wedding invitations to our friends and family. I sat in my car at the post office with the box of invitations in my lap and a pit in my stomach. I asked for spiritual guidance, something I used to do as a child. For some reason, in that moment I reverted back to the comfort of knowing that guidance was available to me.

"Angels, I'm not sure why I have this pit in my stomach or why I'm so nervous…I mean, I know it's a big fucking deal to get married and to be with the same person for the *rest* of my life, so if I'm not supposed to marry this guy, please give me a sign." I trusted that my prayer was heard as I walked into the post office to mail out our wedding invites.

Little did I know how fast the angels work. Two days later, Jaide and I were on the way to my parents' beach house for the day. We were coming up to the street my grandpa lives on, and I got an overwhelming feeling to stop in at his house. He was struggling with dementia, and his health was rapidly declining, so I thought I better stop and visit.

As Jaide ran into the next room to play with her great-grandma, I took a seat on his couch. He sat in his recliner, staring out the window at his boat.

"Hi Grandpa...how are you?"

He greeted me with his usual little smirk and said, "Good—can you help me get my suspenders and socks on? Grandma can't help me." I started helping him, and then suddenly he blurted out, "I'm really glad that I could give Todd that money."

"I'm sorry, what did you say? Todd who?" I asked, praying he wasn't talking about my fiancé.

"YOUR FIANCÉ!" he replied in a stern voice.

"*What* did you give him money for?" I was trying to play it cool, but something told me I was about ready to lose my shit.

"He said he'll pay me the $80,000 back when he sells his rental."

I didn't know whether I was going to crap my pants or throw up on my grandpa's leather couch.

The thing is, I knew about the rental, but I could never get the full story from Todd about it. The only thing I knew was that he put a ton of money into it to flip it, and it was just sitting there collecting dust, heading toward a foreclosure (if this was the case, how did he get a loan for a million-dollar house? I'll never know).

I called Todd as soon as I left my grandparents' house.

"Hi baby, what's up?" he said.

"You borrowed $80,000 from my grandfather and didn't tell me?! You didn't think you needed to discuss it with me prior?!" I jumped right into it.

"It's a business transaction, Stacey," he replied in a very calm, but patronizing, tone.

"A business transaction? I'll show you a business transaction, buddy! Where's the money now?"

"In a bank account," he said.

At that point in the conversation I was so upset that I couldn't see straight. Jaide and I arrived at the beach house, and I briefly filled my mom in and asked if Jaide could stay so I could head back home to get to the bottom of what was going on. I was hoping there was a good explanation for why he needed the money.

It seems that he went to my grandfather and struck up a conversation about the house he was flipping. The idea Todd presented was that when the house was sold, my grandfather would get the money back, but I knew the house was close to being in foreclosure, so that was never going to happen. I couldn't believe my fiancé had taken money from my loving and trusting grandfather.

I got home and found Todd upstairs taking a nap. He never took naps, so this seemed odd. I stormed into the bedroom.

"You need to tell me exactly what's going on. Are you in some sort of financial trouble? Did you think that you couldn't talk to me about it?"

"There's nothing to talk about, and it's none of your business what I need this money for," he said, and rolled over.

Oh, hell no...

DECISION TIME

I spent the next two weeks trying to figure out what I was going to do with the bowl of shit the universe had just handed me.

I was already receiving RSVPs and phone calls from friends and family who were sharing their excitement for our upcoming special day—I just had to act like nothing was wrong. I had already purchased my beautiful wedding dress, and my bridesmaids had already purchased their dresses too. Our extravagant two-week honeymoon to Maui was booked. We had paid a non-refundable $25,000 deposit for the reception at the country club. Not to mention that our wedding planner had worked so hard for months planning a beautiful day, and to whom we had also paid a non-refundable $5,000 fee.

It didn't help that I had to share a house with him. I couldn't eat, sleep, or basically function. I was so angry, confused, scared, and in shock. I was numb. My diet, which consisted of cigarettes, candy, and white wine, didn't help my mental state either. It's no wonder that with all that intense anxiety I lost twenty pounds in only a couple of weeks.

It was like a light switch had flipped off in the relationship. After I found out about the money, there was no finding Todd in the shower with me, changing my razors, or putting toothpaste on my toothbrush. That was fine with me though. I couldn't stand the thought of him, especially sharing a bed with him, so I'd sit outside for the majority of the night, pondering the whole situation. *Was there a chance this was just a business deal? And didn't everyone always joke that married people had less sex?* I wanted to believe those things more than anything, because that would be easier. I wanted to wake up from this nightmare.

The next day I showed up at my friend Amber's workplace to catch up on her break. "Hey, how ya holding up?" she asked.

"I can't marry him. I'm so scared, Amber," I told her as I started to cry. Amber did what she always does—she assured me that everything was going to be okay and that she was going to help me through this.

Amber and I discussed how Todd had everything I'd ever thought was important—nice cars, the best zip code, extravagant vacations—but none of that seemed to matter anymore. What really mattered to me now was setting a good example for my young daughter. I envisioned her being a young woman in her early twenties (about the age she is now) with a look of disappointment on her face upon discovering the truth: that I chose to marry a man, knowing he took advantage of her Bigga Papa, because I didn't have the courage to call off the wedding and I was too worried about what people would think of me. What if she asked me if I would be okay with her being with a man like him? What advice would I give her if she was in this situation?

The answer was clear. It was time to ditch this douche.

I knew what needed to happen, so I went home to give Todd the news.

"I'm done, and I'm moving out this weekend so please don't be here."

"Don't worry. You'll never see me again," he replied calmly, and with that he walked out of the house. His eyes were dead, no emotion at all. His body language and tone had changed the day I found out about the money. I couldn't believe this was the same guy who, just weeks ago, was doing everything for me. Now, he just walked out of my life like I was trash. Thinking back to how he reacted when I called and asked him about the money, it's clear to me that as soon as he got the cash, he was done with me. He got what he needed from my grandfather's pockets.

I sent 250 notes to all the wedding guests letting them know the big day was canceled. At the time, Jaide was camping with her grandparents, and I called her to let her know that we (and Max, too) were moving out of the big house. The next thing to do was gather my soul sisters to help me move back to my condo, which at least had a fresh coat of paint and new carpet.

MOVING DAY

I greeted Amber and Tina at the door. I must have looked like hell because they both stood in the doorway, staring with their eyes wide open.

"You guys want to come in?" I somberly asked.

"Stace, are you okay? You look like you haven't eaten in weeks…and I love you, but have you showered lately?" Tina asked. I just crawled back upstairs to my bedroom floor where I lay back down, curled up in a ball, and continued crying. They sat with me and did their best to bring me some sort of comfort. Tina and Amber expressed how proud they were of me to have the courage and strength to call off my wedding and do what I felt was best for Jaide, regardless of how hard it was going to be. They offered to do whatever they needed to do to help us through this. I pulled myself together, and they got to work packing up all the things I needed to make my condo livable.

There are parts of the moving day that are still a blur. Emotional trauma tends to do this. I didn't know what day it was, let alone where to begin packing, but thankfully my friends had it under control. I would walk in circles in the kitchen with an empty water glass in my hand, not knowing what to do with it.

Amber and Tina took note of my rapidly declining mental state (God bless them) and came up with a simple task that they knew I could mentally handle. It was called the Hanger Game.

"Hey Stace, we got you, girl. Let's see what we can do to make this easier on you. Why don't you be in charge of packing all the hangers? Does that sound good?"

"Yeah," I replied. "Sounds…great."

"Okay, cool. So, here's a hanger—all you need to do is put it in that box in the living room, and then come back."

"Yep, I think I got it."

This game went on all…day…long. I didn't think I had that many hangers, but Amber coordinated the game so that it lasted the majority of the day, keeping me focused on something other than the nightmare I was living (well played, my friend). Meanwhile, Tina and Amber moved couches, dressers, and TVs, and packed up many boxes to go into the U-Haul. Then, they somehow managed to unpack and carry everything up three flights of stairs to my condo—all while I packed and unpacked hangers.

I'm forever grateful for both these ladies.

SERIAL DOUCHEBAG

Remember that Todd told me the money was in a secret bank account? Before I moved out and called things off, I went to his workplace unexpectedly and asked to see the checkbook of this other account the money was in. He was NOT happy. The expenses listed were for stupid things, and to this day, I don't know exactly what he needed that money for. But the lies were extensive. He had put $6,000 of the full amount into our joint account, thinking he could tell me that that money was from my grandfather (to cover the paint and carpet for the condo), and then I would never even find out about the other $74,000. He had every opportunity to tell me the whole story, but he didn't. Even after I found out, if there was no longer anything to hide, why not explain it to me?

Now that I had the checkbook, the next thing I did was catch up with a friend who worked at that bank. She said that Todd had presented a check, in his handwriting, made out to him, and opened up a new account. She said she had noticed my grandfather's name on the check and had specifically mentioned it.

"I notice that you have a joint account with us; did you want to add Stacey to this account too?" she'd asked.

"No, and I also need to have these bank statements sent to my work address, not our home address," he'd replied.

She felt bad, but due to confidentiality restrictions there wasn't really anything else she could do at the time except process his request. This gave me more confidence that breaking things off with him was the right move.

I heard the next week through a friend that he was back with his ex-wife. The nightmare wouldn't stop. I would pull up to pick Jaide up from school and stay in my car so I wouldn't run into them. I also didn't want to face the other parents who knew we'd broken up. I was concerned everyone was talking about me (small town bullshit). One day, Todd showed up at my car and asked to get inside.

"You better talk fast before Jaide hops in and sees your face," I said.

He got into the passenger side. "I'll make this quick. Do you think I could get that ring back?" he asked.

"Let me get this straight, asshole. You owe my family $74,000 and you want the ring back?" I turned to look him straight in the eyes.

"You will *never* see that ring again."

Suddenly, Jaide opened the rear door and hopped into the back seat. She settled into her booster chair, and when she looked up, her smile quickly turned upside down.

"WHAT are you doing in our car?"

Before Todd could respond, I asked Jaide if she had anything she wanted to get off her chest.

"I hate you for what you did to my Bigga Papa and for breaking my mom's heart!"

He just stared through the windshield.

"I don't know what to say."

"How about 'I'm sorry'? Get out of my car, NOW."

He made some snide comment about how he was glad to see that I was still carrying around a chip on my shoulder. It shook me up to see how cold he was, just a week after the breakup, since he had supposedly been so in love with me.

A few weeks went by, and when I drove by our old house on the way to my new job I started noticing this other car that wasn't his ex-wife's. I knew I shouldn't care what he did after we broke up, but he still had my grandfather's money, and I wanted to understand what was really going on with him. Soon, a girlfriend of mine mentioned she'd seen him at church.

"Who is this guy? I asked. "He told me he was an atheist." *Fucking chameleon.*

It turned out that he was dating another woman, this time a platinum blonde who my friend said looked like she belonged on the cover of *Rolling Stone.* A few days later, I pulled up to the tanning salon and spotted a beautiful blonde head out toward her black Escalade. This had to be the same woman, so I jumped out of my car.

"Hey…are you Liz*?" I asked her.

"Yeah, do I know you?"

"No, you don't know me, but I unfortunately know the guy you're dating. Listen, I heard you're a very nice woman, and you go to the same church as a good friend of mine. She mentioned seeing Todd there with you."

"And? Are you Stacey?" She lowered her sunglasses and flashed her blue eyes at me.

"Yes. Did he tell you why we broke up?"

"What he told me is that you were super jealous and possessive, and he had to let you go because your insecurity—"

"Hold it right there. Do I seem insecure?"

"So, you're not insecure?" she asked. *Really? That's what Todd was saying about me?* Of course he was putting me down and trying to make himself look like a victim, instead of admitting that he was a complete and utter con artist douchebag who stole from my grandfather with dementia.

"I'll make this quick. To be very clear, I do not want him back, and I'm not sure what fuckery he's telling you, but he's bad news. You deserve to know the truth, so do what you want with it." I gave her the quick version of what had happened.

"I wish someone had told me about him, because it would've saved me and my daughter a lot of heartache."

"Thank you for telling me this," she said with a smile. Without me going into any detail, she shared an eerily similar concern of hers—about how he was changing her razors and putting toothpaste on her toothbrush.

"Did he do that for you too?" she asked.

"Yes, yes he did."

Soon after that, they broke up.

To add to my heartache, my dad called me to let me know that my grandpa was in the hospital and not doing well. When I arrived, I asked the other family members if they wouldn't mind stepping out so I could have a few minutes alone with my grandpa. I told him that I loved him and thanked him for everything he'd done for Jaide and me. He smiled and squeezed my hand. He'd had a stroke and could barely speak, but managed to ask, "Did you get the money back yet?"

"Grandpa, I promise you I'll get that money back. I'm so sorry that someone I loved and trusted and who I was going to marry did this to you. I just wonder if I'll ever meet a nice guy," I said, as tears streamed down my face.

"You will," he whispered. He passed away a few days later, on the afternoon of April 14, 2007.

Rest assured, my family did get that money back, too. We put a lien on Todd's house, and although he tried to get out of that, ultimately he failed. However, getting the money back was just a tiny piece of getting back to myself and healing my heart.

I was doing forgiveness work and asked my angels if I was ready to come face to face with Todd again. How would I know if I was strong enough? The message I received was when I was ready to face him, I would. Eventually, that day came. I was on a walk, on a quiet street in a beautiful neighborhood, when I noticed a guy getting out of a black Jaguar with his dry cleaning tossed over his shoulder. *OMFG...that looks like Todd. OMG, it is! Quick, look away before he sees it's you.*

Too late. We made eye contact, and he slowly looked away like he didn't know me. I walked right by him with my head held high. It was a big moment for me. I really felt nothing for him. No love. No anger. No more asking, "Why'd you do it, asshole?" Simply...nothing. I had truly moved on.

Not long after that I was talking with a woman I happened to sit next to at a local fundraising event. It didn't take long before she told me her life story. She vented about her dating fails and all the douchebags she was tired of meeting. *Oh, I get it girl.* She also told me about her friend who was going through a similar hard time in the dating scene, but that her situation was way worse. She explained that her friend was dating a guy who couldn't keep his lies straight, and even worse, he had financially side-swiped her.

"Financially side-swiped her?" I asked.

"Yeah, he's like a con artist or something, and my friend said she heard through the grapevine that he did this to another single mom! It's like he has a sick pattern of preying on vulnerable women. What's wrong with these guys?"

How much time do you have? I thought. I pulled my phone out of my purse and did a quick search on Facebook. I pulled up a photo and turned the phone to her.

"Is this him?" I asked her.

"YES! How'd you know?!"

I told her a bit about my story.

"WOW! You should really write a book!"

"Yeah, maybe I will one day."

KNOWLEDGE IS POWER

Todd was in a pattern, too. He would find single women who were wealthy, or who had wealthy family members, and he mindfucked those women (myself included) to make us feel like we owed him something because of his so-called devotion and love. That's on him. If you relate to this story and a guy conned you, don't beat yourself up. It's happened well before you and it's unfortunately going to happen after you. It's up to us to protect ourselves and decide what we allow into our lives. We can't change these guys—only they can change themselves. Unfortunately, a lot of the time they don't see their own faults, or think they have anything to work on.

It might be hard to believe, but maybe, just maybe, these douchebags are shining a light on your subconscious limiting beliefs and patterns, patterns that are linked to your unhealed emotional wounds. After years of personal development and a decade of doing this work, I realized that even though all I wanted was to feel loved, ironically I kept attracting men who reinforced my deep-rooted belief that I was unlovable. Nobody ever told me that I was unlovable, or that I didn't deserve respect, so I have no idea why I had this belief, but I did—and I know I did, because I attracted men who proved my belief right. The same principle applies if, instead, I truly believed that I was good enough, or deserving of being in a loving relationship. If that were the case, then I would have attracted a man (like I eventually did) who proved that belief right. In other words, our inner world creates our outer world.

It's important to pause once in a while and take note of what's going on when there are cycles in your life concerning the types of men you attract (or don't attract), how they treat you, or why they may be ghosting you. If they're controlling, narcissists, con artists, liars, cheaters, men who you feel you need to save, etc., dig a little deeper. When you think back, who was the first person who showed you this behavior? Did this person (or persons) withhold love or acceptance, disrespect you, or tell you you weren't worthy of good things? What kind of example did your parents set when it comes to relationships? Was your mom or dad married multiple times? Did your high school love break your heart? This self-reflection will help you identify the root cause of a belief and help you break the cycle. This repeated pattern may also look like a "break up and make up" cycle with the same ex, which tends to be a manipulative situation and not a healthy relationship.

I was so frustrated with myself when I was stuck in those patterns that in one breath I would say I wanted a nice guy, meet a nice guy, then in the next breath, sabotage the entire thing by finding something wrong with him. Then, I'd be upset that I was single again, and soon find myself dating yet another douchebag. I later learned that this would happen because the energy that I was putting out (negative self-talk, focusing on what wasn't working in my life, complaining about everything, etc.) did not match the energy frequency of the type of high-vibe men that I truly desired. Hence why, when I found myself in a relationship with a genuinely nice guy, it felt "off." I was vibing, more or less, at the bottom of the barrel, so I'm assuming it felt off to them as well.

A perfect example is when, after I had Jaide, I spent a few months dating an awesome guy who didn't mind that I had a newborn (bless his heart). His family was just as kind and welcoming as he was. But of course that relationship ended, and I went back to what felt normal to me—my ex—to try and work things out. If I only knew back then what I know now, that I was being given another opportunity to break the cycle, I could have avoided many more years of heartbreak. The cycle will continue until you become aware of it and change it.

Heal Yourself
RELATIONSHIP PATTERN SELF-INVENTORY
To break the cycle of attracting the same types of people and situations, you first need to uncover what your relationship pattern is. Answer the following questions in your journal to identify some beliefs and ideas that are keeping you stuck:

- What type of men do you typically attract?
- Do you tend to date the same type of men over and over?

- What do you struggle with most in relationships? (For example, jealousy, trust, or codependency.)
- What do you hear most often from men you're dating? (Too needy, too powerful, too controlling, too much, too materialistic, etc.)
- Do you have a pattern of being in a "make up and break up" cycle?
- Do you find yourself dating someone you know you have no future with?
- How do your relationships tend to end?
- What did you learn about relationships growing up?

Now, give yourself a rating for each of the questions below:

- On a scale from one to ten (with ten being the most open), how open are you to seeing things differently?
- On a scale from one to ten (with ten being the most ready), how ready are you to create space for your person to come into your life?

And try this mantra: "I can and will meet my Mr. Right."

Don't believe that yet? Keep reading. I didn't either—until my life changed, thanks to the help I found in the next chapter.

CHAPTER 5

Lightning Strikes Again...and Again

Remember Nick, the chronic cheater? Well, after Nick cheated on me one time too many, I changed my locks so he couldn't get back into my home—or hopefully my life. At this point, a weekend trip to Vancouver, British Columbia, with my girlfriends was in order.

Hayley* and I picked up Jaide from my parents' house on the way home from our girls' weekend.

After we got home, Hayley called me on my landline to make sure we were settled in and everything was okay. She expressed her concern again about Nick, knowing he had displayed obsessive behavior and stalker tendencies toward me. She worried about what would be next with this guy. I assured her that all was well and that I was sure he was busy with one of his many other girlfriends.

At 1:00 a.m., I woke up to the sound of my front door opening and footsteps running toward my bedroom.

"Where is he?!" a voice yelled as the bedroom light turned on. I opened my eyes to see Nick standing at the end of my bed, out of breath and with a look in his eyes that I'll never forget. They were dark and intense, a look only sociopaths have. He looked like he was about to kill someone. Clearly he thought he was catching me in bed with another man. *It's my daughter, you idiot.*

In a panic, I reached over to my nightstand for the cordless phone that, luckily, I had forgotten to return to the kitchen the night before. I started to dial 911, but before I could finish, he snatched the phone out of my hand and stuck it in the back pocket of his jeans.

"Where have you been all weekend?! Who is he?" he screamed in my face. *Oh buddy, you're about to go face to face with Mama Bear.*

"We're taking this conversation to the living room, asshole. In case you didn't notice, there's a toddler asleep in here."

I pushed by him as he tried to grab me. I made a beeline for my Motorola flip phone on the kitchen counter. He jerked it out of my hand and threw it down the hall. For two hours he paced my living room, crying and asking, "Who is he? Please just tell me!" It was inconceivable to him that there was no other man, that I just didn't want him or his bullshit anymore.

"Fine! You want me to leave? I'll leave!" he yelled as he stormed to my front door. *Thank God, it's 3:00 a.m.!*

He was halfway out the door…but instead of leaving, he suddenly turned around and told me he wasn't done talking yet. He backed me into the kitchen and used his muscular body to push me up against the counter as he reached for a butcher knife from the knife block. Then, he held it to his chest. His hand was shaking, his lips were tightly pressed together, and tears ran down his face.

I was crying and screaming bloody murder, begging him to put the knife down.

"If you want to rip my heart out then you can watch me do it right here!"

I had no doubt he was going to turn the knife on me and kill me. I thought, *Oh my God, Jaide is going to find me dead in the morning. I can't do that to her! She needs her mommy! Oh God, please help me!*

Within seconds I felt a calming angelic energy step in and take over me. Words began to flow out of my mouth, words that I couldn't believe I was saying to him, but I just went with it. I heard myself repeatedly tell him, "I love you, and you're right. We need to be together. Let's work this out. Please don't do this."

He slowly put the knife down. As I spoke, his rage seemed to disappear. I assured him everything was going to be okay and that we would talk more the next day, after we both got some sleep. We hugged for a brief moment before I guided him back to my front door.

I don't know how I got to sleep, but finally, I did.

TAKING CONTROL

The next morning, my friend Julie called me to ask about my weekend. She had been very worried previously about Nick's behavior, because one of her cousins had been shot and killed by her ex-fiancé years before. He had displayed behaviors that Nick had also exhibited, and she encouraged me to stay away from him. I had argued that she didn't know Nick, and that he would never actually hurt me or Jaide. However, after the previous night, I knew she had been right before, and I had to admit I was wrong, because I needed her help.

I broke down and told her everything. When I got to the part about my cell phone not being in my bedroom, she asked me why I didn't have a phone in my bedroom at all times. This was back in the days of landlines, and I had a cordless phone in the kitchen of my small condo. That had seemed like plenty. She told me to check and see if I had a phone jack where I could easily add a bedroom phone. To this day, I have no idea why she asked me to do this, but I can't help but think it was a divine intervention. While we were still on the phone, I went and checked to see if there was a phone jack. There was, but a cord was already coming out of the jack. It trailed underneath my nightstand.

"That's strange," I said. I slowly pulled the cord.

There was a recording device.

"Shut the front door! He's been tapping my phone!"

Hayley came over to sit with Jaide (who thankfully was oblivious to what was going on), and Julie and I headed to the police department.

The police officer at the front desk had his feet on the edge of the desk, leaning back in his chair.

"What's up, ladies?" he asked, like it was a social call.

"I found this recording device under my nightstand…my ex put it there," I said, and showed him the machine.

"A recording device?"

After I told him about Nick waving the knife around last night, I finally had his full attention. The cop processed the machine and came back with a big smile on his face.

"This guy just screwed himself. Not only did this device capture the conversation with your friend hours prior and her concern of his behavior toward you, but when you started to call 911 it activated the device again. He forgot to turn it off, so everything from last night was also recorded."

"Oh my God. That whole conversation was recorded?"

"Yes, ma'am."

It sank in. I had ultimate proof from Nick's own mouth that I had begged him to leave. That he was accusing me of cheating. That I screamed and begged him to put the knife down. It even captured him saying he got into my house because he stole a key from my counter when he had stopped by days prior begging me to take him back. That's how he had the ability to barge in, even after I'd changed the locks.

"I wonder how long that recorder was there?" I asked.

"There's not much tape beyond last night, so maybe when you were away on the trip you mentioned. That's probably when he installed the device. So, we can arrest this guy today," the cop said.

Then, the background report came back, and we were floored by how many women had made complaints and filed restraining orders against Nick, including the nineteen-year-old girl who had called my condo looking for him. It was tough to process his pattern of aggression and possessiveness toward women, and yet also his inability to keep his dick in his pants. *Talk about a mindfuck.*

LIGHTNING STRIKES THREE TIMES

I did finally break that Nick addiction, and then my Todd addiction too. To mark the end of that relationship, I dyed my hair from a sunny blond to almost black. That dark color matched how I felt inside. I wanted to disappear. I didn't know how to change my life, but I did know how to change my appearance. And so, once I finished picking up the pieces of my heart, both from Todd and the passing of my grandpa, lightning struck again. This next guy, Jeff*, was a liar like Nick and a con artist like Todd. *Lucky me.*

Jeff was younger than me, which was a first. I had decided that maybe the older guys didn't seem to have it together like I thought they would, so maybe a younger man was the missing piece to the puzzle. I met him at a work event through a girlfriend. As we were getting to know each other, I happened to make note of a handsome coworker sitting at a nearby table. His name was Chris, and I had seen him a few times around the office and at other work events, but I'd never spoken to him. He always seemed pretty quiet, but this time I noticed he was two sheets to the wind. I got an intuitive feeling that he was going through a hard time. I didn't know him well enough to ask, so I let it go and turned my focus back to the young buck I'd just met.

Jeff and I clicked that night. He told me he used to be a pro athlete, and that he was an entrepreneur. He also shared that he didn't have much of a relationship with his dad, who was struggling with mental illness. That made me feel like I really knew something personal about him—how much of it was true is questionable now, in hindsight. After that first night, we made plans to go on a date. However, at the last minute, he canceled. He told me his dog had gotten into a bag of chocolate and was about to die…or maybe he said the dog had already died? I seriously can't remember the exact story, because the guy lied so much that I have no idea what was really true, and to be honest I've decluttered a lot of this old shit from the files in my brain.

One memory I have is when he showed up to a house party that summer wearing a scarf around his neck. My girlfriend yelled out,

"Hey buddy, what's with the scarf? It's hot out." Jeff mumbled some weird excuse. I wanted to crawl under the table. Something was wrong, but I didn't want to pay attention to what it was.

Fast forward eight months, and I still hadn't met his family. Finally, he set up a dinner out so that I could meet them. That night, we were meeting them at a restaurant, and they were already inside waiting for us. Jeff pulled up to the valet and turned to give him the keys, and there it was. On his neck I saw a big, red hickey.

"WHY do you have a hickey on your neck?" I asked, my nostrils flared in anger. I sure as hell didn't put it there.

"Why are you bringing this shit up when you're about to meet my family for the first time? Of course you ruin tonight, Stacey!" He tried to put my question back on me, like I shouldn't have even brought it up—typical gaslighting technique. That pissed me off even more. He got his keys back from the valet, and we left. I was silent the whole way home and didn't bring it up again. I should have, but I didn't want to rock the boat. My mental state at this point was fragile, and I couldn't imagine going through another breakup. I sucked it up and told myself I must have been seeing things, so I dropped it. I'm sure he enjoyed that because he didn't want to be questioned, but part of me thinks he was happy to have that fight as an excuse to leave and not introduce me to his family. Was he afraid that I would figure out what a lying douche he was?

Not too long after that night, I found an email from a girl. He said she was just a friend. It didn't sound like just a friend to me, but it wasn't hard proof of anything, either. I recalled that time he wore the scarf in the summertime—was it because he had another hickey that he didn't want me to notice? Because I had met Jeff through a mutual friend, I kept thinking that maybe he really was telling me the truth—because how could my friend be friends with a total liar? My gut was telling me something was off, but I didn't trust myself to make good decisions (for obvious reasons), and part of me thought I was making stuff up in my head. After Nick and Todd, I thought I just had trust issues. Understandably.

A few weeks later, Jeff went out of town for a business meeting and told me his grandpa would be joining him. He knew how close I was to my grandparents, so I thought it was sweet. I spoke to him that afternoon, and he shared with me that his grandpa had showed up at 5:30 a.m. and packed them egg salad sandwiches, Frito chips, and an apple for the road. They were about to head into a meeting when he called me, so he said he would call me later. Hours passed with no call, so I decided to call him to see what time he was heading home and whether or not I would see him.

I still don't know how this happened (maybe the angels intervened again), but instead of me calling his cell phone, I actually called his landline, and his grandpa answered. Assuming I had called Jeff's cell phone, I said, "Hi, this is Stacey. I hope I'm not interrupting your meeting, but is Jeff available?" I thought it was strange that his grandpa would be answering his cell phone, but I thought he might be busy taking care of one of his "big business deals."

"Who is this?" he asked in a crabby old man voice. I raised my voice, thinking that maybe he was hard of hearing.

"This is Stacey, Jeff's girlfriend."

"I've never heard of you. Jeff isn't here. He left this morning, and I haven't seen him all day." Click.

I looked down at my phone—what the actual fuck just happened?! This is when I realized I had accidentally called Jeff at home, and not his cell phone. Lies are like turds, the bad ones float to the top. *Wow. That son of a bitch!* His grandpa had never heard of me, he didn't know Jeff was seeing anyone, he didn't know anything about a meeting with Jeff. And earlier Jeff went into great detail about the kind of sandwich his grandpa had supposedly brought him? This was the tipping point that proved I wasn't going crazy. My intuition was right—if his lips were moving, he was lying.

I called Jeff's cell phone next, and he answered.

"Hey, how'd the meeting go?" I asked.

"Good, really good! Sounds like we got the deal," he said.

"Oh, that's great…how's grandpa doing?"

"Goooood, why?"

"I know he's goooood because he's not with you, you lying piece of shit!" I said, and slammed the phone down. After I hung up, I got on my computer and did some research. I noticed there was no online proof of his supposedly elite athletic career. None at all. *Why didn't I play FBI sooner?* There were no pictures, no news articles for college or pro teams of any kind, nor was there any proof he owned his business. The business existed, sure, but it wasn't in his name. When Jeff got home, we continued our conversation, and he did his best to backpedal as fast as he could.

"I have cancer," he blurted out.

His cover story for the lie about the trip with his grandfather was that he was getting cancer treatments in secret and didn't want his family or anyone to worry. He said he'd been seeing a specialist in California. I thought that was odd— why would he go out of state?

When he returned from that trip, after supposedly receiving cancer treatment, he looked just the same. His complexion was great, he had no bags under his eyes, or muscle weakness. He was strong and energetic. We went out drinking and partying like he wasn't even sick. I knew then that there was just no way he was seriously ill. And it seemed weird to me that he would lie about something like cancer; not just to me, but also to the mutual friend who had introduced us.

Some time later, I was on a business trip and tried calling Jeff numerous times. He didn't answer, and I knew I couldn't take one more minute of his lies. I texted him, "Go fuck yourself and your lies. I'm done." Mature, I know. But it was a clean breakup after that, because he had to have known that I was on to his lies. And sure enough, a few weeks later, when our mutual friend called me to see how I was doing since the breakup, she confided that Jeff's friends were also doubting his cancer story.

Even though I turned out to be right and not completely crazy, I didn't feel better. I shut down, and things went dark. *Really* dark. It was the lowest point of my life. I wondered if I would ever meet a guy who would be straight with me. It hurt to breathe, and I was so depressed. I didn't know what was wrong with me and wondered if this was how it was going to be for the rest of my life, just going from one liar to the next. I was hoping my grandpa was right; that one day I would meet a nice guy.

My drinking after work got worse. I needed something to help me cope with the intense anxiety and the deep sadness I was struggling with. I so badly wanted someone to take the pain away.

"The best way to get over one guy is to get under another one," another friend suggested to me while we were at a bar.

I thought it over for a second, but rejected the idea. *That may have worked in the past, but that's not what I need right now. Plus, it's only a quick fix. There has to be a better way.*

Experiencing these uncomfortable emotions is cause to call up your true friends, the ones you can trust, so you don't go through it alone—especially when it feels like your heart's literally being pulled out and you think the pain will never go away. Hopping in the sack with another man will only cause more emotional pain down the road. Sorry sister, but it takes longer than a few minutes to heal your heart. Unfortunately, in order for the pain to go away, you must feel it to heal it, so you don't take it into that next relationship and get the same lesson. This is how you will break the cycle.

Sometimes the only thing to say after a breakup is "This fucking sucks." As hard as it is, the best thing to do is to process your emotions instead of looking outside yourself for comfort, such as buying new clothes or a new car, jumping into a relationship, or falling back to a familiar fuck. Those things will not prevent you from feeling the pain; they will only prolong the healing process.

If I had taken the time to heal my heart and focus on self-love after each breakup, I truly believe that I could have avoided a lot of heart-ache and emotional trauma. Love yourself enough to take the time to grieve. Become your own best friend and work through your emotions before getting into another relationship. You and your next beau will be happy you did.

Plus, for readers already in a relationship and feeling like you have some healing to do, it's never too late. You will only improve your current relationship with this work.

CONNECT THE DOTS

There is one common denominator in each of my dating fails: me.

The more I learned about energy and the Law of Attraction, the more I started to connect the dots in my life. It was a hard pill to swallow, realizing that I was the one common denominator in each of my relationships. To be clear, I sure as hell didn't deserve to be treated like that by those men, but if I'd already known the tools that I'm sharing in this book, maybe I could've prevented myself from going through those situations, or staying in the relationships for so long. It took some time for me to learn how to forgive myself for not doing better in the past and to accept it deep within myself that I could change my future.

In the last chapter, we talked about how your beliefs impact what you attract into your life, and situations that continue to show up are nothing more than deep-rooted wounds from your past experiences that are still waiting to be healed. You may be thinking, *No way! I dealt with that years ago!* Well, that may be partially correct, but if you had truly healed it, it wouldn't be showing up again. We can spend hours talking through it with a girlfriend, or years sitting on a couch in a counselor's office. But the problem is, if we don't deal with the root cause of the issue, we stay stuck in the pattern.

Do you find yourself saying, "Of course that happened!" when something goes wrong? Look at the "of course" part. It binds you to a limiting belief that is not serving you. In this sense, "of course" means you expected it to happen. I used to say, "Of course this guy screwed me over and is a cheater and a liar"—really?! What I should have been saying was, "Of course, this guy screwed me over and is a cheater and a liar—because he got the message from the universe that I had a deep-rooted belief that this was all I deserved!" Or, "Of course this guy repeatedly canceled on me, because he got the universal message that I didn't even like spending time with myself!"

This may be hard to hear, but it's not about the men who broke your heart. Yes, he is (or was) a total douchebag, and how he treated you is absolutely not okay. I'll give you that. But maybe, just maybe, these guys are (unconsciously, of course) trying to help you heal a much deeper story, belief, or an inner-child wound, if you're open to seeing it this way.

I know this is probably not what you were expecting to learn in this book, but stay with me.

Heal Yourself
BREAK THE CYCLE

If you feel that all you do is attract douchebags into your life, that is a pattern that you can change. To make that shift, you must be open and willing to do the work on yourself.

Here are some questions to ask yourself:

- What am I bringing to this repeated pattern?
- What is the belief underneath that's keeping me stuck in this cycle?
- What story do I have on repeat? (Always ghosted, always cheated on, always taken advantage of, always giving too much, etc.)
- Am I breaking cycles in my family, or repeating them? (Clue: Did you hear your parents yell at each other growing up, and now that is how you communicate in your own relationships?)

As you answer these questions, you'll uncover radical self-awareness and self-accountability. Own up to why you are attracting these unhealthy relationships so that you can eventually attract a better-quality man.

Let's go deeper into this process.

Ask yourself, *Do I feel I deserve a loving relationship?* If you answered "no" to that question, it's okay. Let's find out what's going on. Ask yourself, *What old emotional wounds do I need to heal?* Answering this question thoughtfully will help you begin to heal the wounds these guys exploit. Once they're healed, those guys won't be able to hurt you the same way even if they try, because you will no longer be vulnerable in that place.

Here are the three steps of deep work I did to uncover the deep-rooted beliefs I was carrying and change them, in order to change how I would show up and who showed up in my life:

Step 1: Start with your parents and what you learned about relationships as a child. How were you treated by your parents? How was love shown to you?

Step 2: What did you learn about your self-worth from your ex-boyfriends? Your friendships? The guys we date and our friendships can both affect how we feel about ourselves.

Step 3: What have you learned about your value from your job? If you have a limiting belief that you are unimportant or not good enough, you may seek approval from your boss, get freaked out if he or she is upset with you, and attract bosses who don't appreciate all your hard work (i.e., you're unimportant at work) and make you feel like you're not good enough for that big promotion or raise.

See how this works? Our beliefs don't just affect our dating situation, they create a ripple effect that spreads to other areas in our life. I share this because if you're having a hard time figuring out your belief system, take a look at other areas of your life—examine who or what is triggering you to believe these untrue and harmful things about yourself and what you deserve in your life.

CHAPTER 6

"You're Not a Victim" — Say What?

If you want to change your life, change your energy.
- Joe Dispenza

For most of my life, I've been in counseling. It started when I was fifteen years old, when I was sent to a therapist for treatment of an eating disorder. I was struggling with bulimia and depression. I learned that I felt out of control and didn't know how to process my emotions, which led me to seek control in other areas. The solution at the time was to put me on an antidepressant.

When I was trying to work things out with Nick, the therapist told me, "You're like a frog that doesn't know when to jump out of a pot of boiling water." Okay. That was about as helpful as being filled with pills that made me feel numb as a teen, but I suppose he was right. I didn't jump out because I would hold on to the good I saw in that person, even if it wasn't in either of our best interests.

Maybe all of this could have been avoided if I had a better understanding of my emotions and how to process them in a healthy way as a child. I don't know about you, but I didn't grow up in a family that sat around talking about their feelings. Once I learned more about how my parents were raised, it helped me understand both of them better and gave me insight into their parenting style. To be clear, they weren't bad parents at all, they were just raised in a different generation with different norms. Once I recognized this, I was able to bless and release them from the story I was telling myself, and instead see that I was being given an opportunity to do things differently with my own parenting style.

I will always be committed to helping Jaide avoid waking up a hot mess, like I did at thirty-five. When she was a teenager, our communication got a little hairy. That is when I created the method of "Mom A or Mom B." Together, we determined that if she wanted my two cents, she would ask for Mom A, but if she just wanted to vent and needed someone to listen to her, then Mom B would step in. This technique worked great and saved us from many fights (and still does). As hard as it was for me to be Mom B sometimes, I found it to be one of the most beneficial things I could have done as a parent.

I found this different way of being and processing my emotions when I went to my hairdresser after the breakup with Jeff. She had suggested a certain therapist to some other clients of hers, and this therapist was able to help them figure out why they were attracting certain kinds of men. That sounded like EXACTLY the answer to my biggest question. I called to make an appointment, spoke to the therapist directly, and was offered a one-hour session.

"You don't understand. I'm going to need more than an hour," I said.

"No, an hour will be plenty of time," he replied. I took what was offered and figured he'd give me more time when he saw how broken I was.

NEW THERAPIST, NEW APPROACH

When the appointment came, this new therapist made it clear that he didn't want to camp out in my past, so he went straight to moving me forward. In that first session, he lasered in with more of a life coach approach, instead of the usual "tell me everything" saga, where you can spend hours rehashing every little thing from your childhood. I told him I was tired of feeling broken-hearted, and something needed to change in my life, but I didn't know how to start.

It was hard to swallow the fact that I was the one common denominator in each of my dating fails. There was no way around it. I could no longer blame the men for the shit show I'd lived for so many years. I had to admit to myself that I had played a part too, and now it was time to focus on cleaning up my own mess. I know, I know—they were lying, cheating dicks, but the reality is I tolerated their behavior for far too long, and I ignored many warning signs and continued to show up for more. That's on me, not them.

The question I had for the therapist was, "Why?" This is when I got curious, because I knew I couldn't change something that I wasn't aware of. I started examining my inner world and became extremely open to seeing things differently and on a much deeper level.

"You want to know why—right now?" he asked.

I assumed it would take weeks and months to figure that out—after all, I'd been living it my entire life. "Go for it," I said.

"You're not a victim," he stated simply. He went on to say that in his practice of helping women figure out why they kept attracting the same men, it had to do with transitioning us from a victim mindset to an empowered one.

Okay, I didn't immediately go, "Thanks, doc. All better now!" I had to understand more about what was going on with me in my inner world; why I felt like I was a victim and why these guys were doing all this stuff to me.

"What if these men were showing you what you need to improve on? What if I told you these men were holding up a mirror to show you what you had in common with them?"

"Well, considering I would never tap someone's phone, lie about having cancer, or take advantage of an eighty-year-old man, I'm not sure what I would possibly have in common with any of these dudes," I said.

"From what I can tell, you're right. You wouldn't do any of those things, so let's break this down," he said. *Please do.*

He explained to me that even though I wasn't a pathological liar like Jeff, maybe his lies were mirroring the lie I was telling myself that I could handle my emotional pain on my own, or the lie I was telling others that I was okay, when really I felt like I was dying inside. Not too many people knew the depression that I was struggling with at the time. I was always the strong woman who got through the tough times and was the queen of saying things like, "I've got this. I don't need anyone, *especially* a man. I've been through worse than this. Next. Game over, thanks for playing."

He explained to me that even though I wasn't a serial cheater or a stalker like Nick, maybe the mirror he was holding up for me was to show me that I needed to have stronger boundaries, improve my own mental state, and increase my self-love and self-respect. *Ouch.*

The therapist zeroed in on the fact that, even though I wasn't a con artist writing checks from an old man's checkbook like Todd, maybe he was showing me how to live within my means, have a better relationship with money, or that there are more important aspects in a relationship than material things. *Bingo.*

This meant I pretty much had no boundaries, which left me wide open to receive whatever came my way. The core concept was that I needed to BE the energy that I wanted to attract—for a guy to be truthful, then I would have to be truthful with myself and others. Here are a few more insights:

- If I want a man to unconditionally love and respect me, then I have to unconditionally love and respect myself.
- If I want a man to respect my boundaries, then I need to know what my boundaries are and respect them myself.
- If I want a man to see my worth, then I need to see my worth.
- If I want a man to love every ounce of me, then I need to stop putting myself down with negative self-talk and start to love every ounce of myself—the good, the bad, and the ugly.

In general, I'd been living life with the belief that I wasn't worthy of love and wasn't important. That's why I was attracting men who kept proving those beliefs right. The answer was so simple, but it also made complete sense.

When my new therapist gave me this insight, I felt hopeful for the first time in a long time.

IT'S AN INSIDE JOB

In addition to seeing the therapist and staying focused on my new way of thinking and being, I started working with his wife, who was a Certified Energy Healer. I had never heard of an energy healer, but I knew that my "energy" was low, so I was open to anything that would help me turn my life around. In this partnership, I would have a counseling session with my therapist to talk about the emotional triggers that had come up since our last visit and how to work through them, then I would have a session with his wife to clear the energy. This technique moved the needle for me. I'd leave my sessions feeling emotionally lighter, go back to work, and start practicing what I'd learned.

I had the perfect case study to put my new energy skills to work. There was this woman at my office who had it out for me. I wasn't sure what her problem was, but she triggered me all the time with her snide comments and unfriendly behavior. By triggered, I mean she made my blood boil. I judged her, talked mad shit about her, and quite frankly couldn't stand her. With the help of my therapist, I wondered what she was teaching me by triggering me. I tried to figure it out, since the Law of Attraction is "like attracts like," but I wasn't trying to ruin my coworkers' lives. I wondered: *What mirror could she possibly be holding up for me?*

Then it dawned on me. I remembered that there had been a time in the past when I wasn't showing up as the best version of myself at work either. I had to be honest about what was upsetting me about this woman—her behavior was pointing out something I didn't like about myself. When I recognized that she was acting as a mirror, reflecting a part of me that I wasn't proud of, I was able to become thankful that she showed me what I needed to work on and forgive that part of myself. In fact, after this realization, she didn't make me feel angry anymore and I stopped caring about how she was acting at all. I *cleared* that trigger.

Soon I could walk past her in the office and not get upset, no matter what look she gave me or what snide comment she made. I would just say, "Good morning." At first, she ignored me, but I didn't care. I continued to be friendly. After a while, she started to give me a mumbled "Good morning," in reply. Even with everything that had happened between her and I, I reached out to her when her brother unexpectedly passed away. I didn't expect a response back from her, but my heart told me it was the right thing to do, so I did it. She may have needed to know that someone, even if it was me, cared about her during a difficult time. It didn't matter how she had treated me in the past. What mattered to me was that I was showing up in the world as the best person I could be. I was shocked that I received a kind response in return, thanking me for thinking of her. This was a start of lasting friendship neither one of us expected.

That's how powerful this work is. I had forgiven myself for being bitchy to other people in the past, and I stopped being an energetic match for the same behavior. What we put out into the world is what we get back. It's like a boomerang. Her attitude eventually changed to match my new friendly one. She got the universal message that "Stacey's safe to be friends with." What we focus on expands, so see the best in others and others will see the best in you. Also, be sure to acknowledge when you are no longer triggered by someone. It means the past issues are resolved and the negative energy has been cleared.

Act like the people in your life who irritate you are props. They have been brought into your life (unbeknownst to them) to help you heal a belief, an emotional wound, or an old story, big or small. When I really started implementing this way of thinking into my everyday life, whether it was with the guy I was dating, my daughter, family members, or the coworker who (I thought) was trying to ruin my life by showing up every day with her bitchy pants on, I found my life became easier and more manageable. Not only did the situations magically dissolve when I chose to see the lesson underneath, but the people involved seemed to shift their behavior as well. I applied this method when interacting with my boss, who wasn't the easiest person to work for, but by examining the story underneath my trigger of how he spoke to me I was able to heal a deeper belief I had about myself—that I was not smart enough or good enough. I quietly thanked him for showing me that I had this deep-rooted belief about myself. I swear the next day his tone changed—or was it because I changed my tone about him?

HEAL YOUR PAST AND THE CURRENT ISSUE WILL FADE

Recently, I helped a client, Allie*, process some emotions this way. She had a great date with a guy she met, so he asked her out again. However, he never called back to confirm a time and ghosted her. She became inconsolable. Over a guy she saw once.

I knew there had to be something more underneath the story for her to be this upset. I asked her what this reminded her of, and she said she felt the same way when, as a child, her dad repeatedly didn't show up for his visitations. Her dad ghosted her as a little girl.

"The universe can't send you the really good guy until you heal the stuff about your dad," I gently said. This memory made her feel like she wasn't important enough, just like her dad did. The guy who ghosted her gave her the opportunity to heal her wounded inner child. Did this guy know that he was helping her heal something way deeper? Absolutely not. He was just a prop who helped the old wound come to the surface to be blessed and released. I suggested that Allie read *Radical Forgiveness* that night. The book that had started my healing and forgiveness journey started hers, too.

Think about how you can use these techniques when you're triggered. Imagine what your dating life would be like if, instead of taking everything to heart, you looked at it as an opportunity for personal growth? What if how he chose to treat you had nothing to do with you personally, and was more about healing a deeper wound, story, or belief about your past or childhood? Imagine what you would feel like if you were broken up with and, instead of internalizing it and thinking there must be something wrong with you, you honored your feelings, processed the pain, and discovered the wisdom in the wounds? It may sound unrealistic, but these are things I wish my younger self had known—it would've saved me a lot of tears, frustration, and anguish.

SHIFT TO "IT'S HAPPENING *FOR* ME," NOT "*TO* ME"

When someone does something that makes your emotions kick into overdrive, that's a signal pointing you to a deeper wound that is wanting to come to the surface to be heard and acknowledged. This knowledge is important because you can't change something you're not aware of. I couldn't change the type of guys I was attracting because I wasn't aware enough to understand that they were coming into my life to trigger me, to bring up something that I needed to heal or improve.

The only caveat to this work is you must be open to seeing things differently and be willing to shift your mindset from feeling like a victim to being grateful for the lesson. It's shifting your mindset from "Why is this happening TO me?" to "Why is this happening FOR me?"

Our emotions are always telling the story of what is going on inside us, so it's important to pay attention to what is going on outside us as well. Your emotions are always trying to get your attention, not get you to ignore them. We know when we're happy, and we're even more aware when we're dealing with an uncomfortable emotion.

Heal Yourself

AWARENESS, MINDSET, GRATITUDE HEALING METHOD

Over time, I noticed a method that I had unconsciously created as I used all these new healing tools, such as energy and understanding my emotional vibrations and how they impact who and what I attract in my life. The truth is, even though I've done a lot of healing work over the last decade, things still come up that trigger old wounds that I have to figure out and work through. I do that in a three-step healing process: awareness, mindset, and gratitude.

Here's how the AMG method works:

STEP ONE: AWARENESS

I'm triggered. That's when I feel a low-vibe emotion like sadness, anger, shame, fear, discouragement, worry, frustration, or overwhelm. Those feelings come up when there's something in the past that I need to release and learn from. So, I have to be aware of when that happens so that I can rise up and not stay in these emotions for very long. Without that awareness, I risk staying in those negative emotions and letting them control me.

STEP TWO: MINDSET

Once I'm aware of the low-vibe emotion that is triggering me, I have a choice of how I want to frame the situation. Do I want to see it as "Why is this happening *to* me?" (i.e., the victim mindset that will keep me stuck in the negative emotion), or do I want to choose to ask "Why is this happening *for* me?" (i.e., an empowering mindset that will help me heal an emotional wound and rise to a positive emotion and better outcome).

This step in the process is how I choose to find the wisdom in the wounds from the moment I'm triggered. Otherwise, it may take me a week to shift my mindset and develop awareness of how my low-vibe emotions are affecting me. This inner work isn't easy, but it's worth it. Honor how you're feeling, and if you need some time to process something like anger or sadness, that is totally fine. Feeling is healing. What *isn't* healing is ignoring uncomfortable emotions hoping they will just go away. Unfortunately, it doesn't work like that. Give yourself permission to feel how you are feeling, but be sure to give yourself a deadline for when you'll return to this step to do the work and discover the hidden truth underneath the trigger. If not, what you resist will persist. The negative emotion will keep you stuck in repeated patterns if you don't resolve them within yourself.

Here are some questions I ask myself to move through this step. I suggest that the next time you're triggered, journal your responses to these questions to help bring to the surface what the trigger is really about:

- What emotion am I feeling right now? (Awareness)
- How am I going to choose to see this situation? (Mindset)
- Have I felt like this before? If so, when and with who? (Recognizing repeated patterns)
- What is this situation trying to teach me? What is this emotional trigger *really* about? (Finding wisdom in the wounds)

The idea is that when you're in a low-vibrational state, awareness kicks in to give you an opportunity for personal growth and allows you to move into a mindset to observe your emotions with curiosity. Then, you can identify your triggers and why this is happening "for you" and see what happened in your past that's coming up again. With this understanding, you can shift to gratitude and start healing.

The goal with this step is to shine a light on what is underneath, not to spend more energy on "fixing" what came up. Remember, we do not need to be fixed. All of us are perfectly imperfect. It's simply recognizing the hidden pain and then moving on to the third step: gratitude.

STEP THREE: GRATITUDE

In this step, I recognize that the emotional trigger that came up is giving me an opportunity to be grateful for what this situation is bringing up to help me heal, release, or improve. Gratitude is a high-vibe positive emotion, and it's the final step in my new way of thinking, which I call "Thank You for Showing Me." I believe that being grateful for the lessons, no matter how uncomfortable they seem, played a major role in how I transformed my life. I couldn't stay sad or angry for long if I felt grateful that this emotional trigger happened in order to improve my life.

Here are a few examples of how to apply the "Thank You for Showing Me" method, whether you're single, dating, in a long-term relationship, or even married.

What if you get triggered because you can't seem to get a date?
Thank you for showing me that I DO want to be in a relationship, and that I need to work on taking steps toward finding love.

What if you get triggered because a guy never called you back?
Thank you for showing me that you aren't the guy for me.

What if you get triggered because you've been with a partner for years who won't put a ring on it?
Thank you for showing me that I need to spend less time worrying about if I'm good enough for you to marry, and more time wondering if YOU'RE good enough for ME to marry.
OR
Thank you for showing me that I DO want to get married one day, because I'm a catch and if you don't see that, peace out!

What if you get triggered because your guy doesn't make you a priority in your relationship?
Thank you for showing me that I need to focus less on you making me a priority, and more on me making myself a priority.

What about when you find yourself being triggered because you feel like you're always the one who has to do everything in the relationship?

Thank you for showing me that I need to have stronger boundaries, as well as work on expressing that I need help around the house and with the kids.

OR

Thank you for showing me this is a repeated pattern; that I am always doing everything for a man and not getting anything in return.

What if you find out your man is a total douchebag?
Thank you for showing me what kind of man I DON'T want to be with!

When you can feel even one ounce of gratitude when you get triggered, you are working with the universe to stop bringing you situations that aren't good for you and starting to create space for what you truly desire.

The goal of the AMG method is to focus on having a positive mindset and look within when you notice that you're experiencing uncomfortable negative emotions. If you have a positive mindset, the more likely you are to experience high-vibe energy and attract better dates, more meaningful friendships, financial abundance, success, joy, love, and overall happiness in your life.

On the flip side, if you choose to focus on everything that's going wrong in your life, the more likely you are to experience negative energy and attract even more unwanted situations to complain about. You know the saying "When it rains, it pours," so you may experience unfulfilling dates (if any at all), issues in your romantic relationships, drama with friends, conflict with family members and coworkers, or even conflict with your children if you're a parent.

This is the Law of Attraction. Simply put, "like attracts like." If you're not wanting to attract negative situations or people, then you must shift your energy and do your best to get to higher ground. If you're tired of things not working out for you in life, start focusing on what *is* working. If you're tired of your kids misbehaving or making poor choices, start focusing on what they are doing right. If you're tired of dealing with a partner or a friend who makes you feel unworthy or unimportant, find ways to make *yourself* feel worthy and important. Words have legs, so pay close attention to the type of words you use. The universe is always listening, so when you're venting about something, be sure to end on a positive.

This is a moment-by-moment process, and it requires awareness of uncomfortable low-vibe emotions and lots of practice to shift your mindset and find the lesson. However, you'll find that the more you do it, the more you train your brain, and the easier it gets to shift your energy and bounce from a low-vibe negative emotion to a high-vibe positive one.

When you recognize that you're stuck in a "Why is this happening *to* me?" vibe and are willing to shift your mindset to "Why is this happening *for* me?" instead, celebrate that shift upward! It's not easy to shift your mindset when you're in a funk, so be sure to acknowledge that you made the choice to shift your energy. There may be days when you're feeling grateful, and in a split second you see a post on social media that irritates you—that's okay! Take a deep breath, acknowledge the shift of where you're at, and apply the AMG method any time you get triggered or feel stuck in a low-vibe energy so that you can shift the direction of your life.

Lastly, take a few minutes each day to write about three to five things that you're grateful for in order to cultivate an attitude of gratitude. These items don't have to be anything fancy—the key is to focus on the good in your life so that more good things show up.

RAISE YOUR VIBRATION JOURNAL EXERCISE

Here are some journal prompts to help you work with your emotions so you can attract higher vibrations in your life—especially in romantic relationships. For a whole week, pay attention to what emotions show up throughout your day and how often they appear, and journal about what you're doing or what's going on in your life. Here are some specific questions to get you started:

What best describes your mood when you are...
- Getting up in the morning?
- On your commute to work?
- At the office, or on Zoom calls?
- Going out to eat? On a date? With friends? With your parents or siblings? With your children (if you're a parent)?

This is a great tool to help you become aware of your emotions and take responsibility for the energy frequency you are bringing to any given situation. This will allow you to make any changes to how you show up in the world so you can attract more joy, love, peace, and abundance in every area of your life.

CHAPTER 7

The Blame Game

I had no idea how much I blamed my parents for how bad I felt about my life until I started unpacking my emotional baggage. The truth is, my parents never told me that I was unworthy of love or respect—actually, it was the complete opposite, and they never treated each other the way my ex-boyfriends treated me. The connection between my family and how I felt about myself is deeper and murkier than that.

My parents met in elementary school. They began dating in high school, got married the summer after my mom graduated and my dad returned from the Coast Guard, and immediately started a family. I never heard my parents argue, except the time when Mom cried because Dad said they couldn't have tile for the kitchen remodel. Dad wisely took note of Mom's out-of-the-ordinary reaction and figured that she must've been having a rough day raising three small children—she got her tile. My mom heard her parents argue a lot growing up, and she said she secretly wished that they would just get a divorce, so she probably took extra care to ensure that we never had the same experience. However, the importance they placed on not arguing in front of us meant that, as my therapist back in the day said, I didn't develop ways to have an argument in a healthy way. *Parents can never win.*

My parents had three kids and built their first house by the time they were both twenty-four. My dad was a successful business owner who worked hard and provided more than enough for myself and my two older siblings. We had food on the table, clothes, cars to drive, and enjoyed many family vacations together.

It's interesting to me that, even though I was extremely fortunate growing up, maybe there were times that I needed a hug, or to hear "I love you." My family wasn't the lovey-dovey type, and we never told each other how we felt. If my siblings and I fought, my parents made us sit on the couch and hold hands. It was brutal. My sister wouldn't let me play with her hair, so I would wait for my dad to come home from work after a long day and he'd let me put barrettes in his hair while we watched *Monday Night Football*, or *The Muppet Show* if I was lucky. I looked forward to quality time with my dad.

BEING MISUNDERSTOOD

I never felt like I belonged in my family, and always felt like the black sheep. I've never done the things that society or my parents have expected of me, like going off to a four-year college program—nope; I'll get my degree online while climbing the corporate ladder and being a single mom. What about getting married to my high school sweetheart and having a baby? No thanks—I'll have an unplanned blessing when I'm twenty-one and wait until I'm thirty-eight to get married to a man who deserves me. Go to work to make someone else money and retire at sixty-five? Definitely not—I'll leave the corporate world and start a couple of businesses.

I asked my mom what I was like as a little girl, and here's what she said: "You were always a free spirit, you did what you wanted; headstrong but very caring—oh, and you loved to garden in the buff," she recalled, laughing.

"Is there anything else you can remember, Mom? Prior to me turning into a teenager and making your life a living hell? I need the deets for my book."

STACEY DEWALD

"I do remember you running into the house sobbing when you were about three years old because your imaginary friend, 'Bob,' got hit by a car in front of our house and died." *RIP Bob.*

"Okay, on that note, this interview is over," I laughed. Well, she didn't seem to think I didn't belong, so why did I?

Since I had this story of feeling like I didn't belong in my family, I was really good at collecting evidence that this was indeed the case. I would go to family gatherings and 90% of the time I would leave early, because I was either annoyed or extremely upset by the things they said or joked about. Looking back, I truly don't think they were trying to be dicks, but my outlook at that time was to collect evidence that I was an outsider, the odd one out. The story of not feeling like I belonged in my family ran deep. I took everything very personally. It felt like the truth, so I believed it. I had to blame my pain on something, right? I don't know why I came up with these stories and beliefs that I wasn't worthy of love, or that I didn't belong in my family, but I did. However, the more I write this book, the more healing I'm doing. I hope you are too.

Since both of my parents worked, I would come home after school by myself, only eight years old and in second grade. Maybe you could call me a latchkey kid, except we lived on three acres, so if I had ever needed help, I would have had to ride my bike to a neighbor's house.

My mom and my sister have always had a special bond, leaving me feeling left out. For my tenth birthday, I recall sitting at the table with the cake in front of me, candles ablaze, and waiting for my family to join me. My mom and sister were talking with each other in the kitchen, my brother was at his friend's house, and my dad was out in the barn, feeding the cows. Things like that might seem small, but over time they added up, and acted as more evidence that I wasn't important to my family. The little girl in me knows now that my family didn't intentionally do that to hurt me. This was just my little farm girl's perception, through distorted lenses, of what I thought was the truth.

I always wondered why my dad never told me he loved me. I asked my grandma if he ever said it to her. She said, "No, but I know he does,

74

and he loves you too." I tried to communicate this to him at age thirteen, asking him (no doubt in a snotty teenage voice) if he loved me, and if so, why he never said so. Needless to say, it didn't go as planned. I was beyond blessed with my upbringing, but maybe I needed more than material things to feel loved.

To make matters worse, I also had a belief that my voice didn't matter, and I had a fear of failure, so I didn't want the spotlight—EVER. Although I played volleyball, I quit my freshman year because I didn't like performing in front of people, or wearing the uniform that consisted of hideous brief underwear-style shorts (as if my body image issues weren't bad enough). I even misspelled "against" in the third grade spelling bee tryouts so I didn't have to compete and stand on a stage in front of a crowd. And don't even get me started about the anxiety I struggled with prior to every single pep assembly in high school—I was afraid I might get called on to do something silly in front of my peers. The thought of people laughing at me reminded me of being teased as a child.

DON'T LET ME DIE

Ten months after I got my driver's license, I was driving to my after-school job. A few car lengths ahead, a car was merging onto the busy highway and collided with me as he shot across the lanes, causing me to spin out of control and eventually crash into the guardrail. The impact jolted me to the left, causing my head to slam against the window. I could hear my tires screeching as I headed toward oncoming traffic on the other side of the bridge. I remember screaming at the top of my lungs, "GOD, PLEASE DON'T LET ME DIE!!" I closed my eyes tight, gripped my steering wheel, and hoped I wouldn't feel anything if I were killed.

Miraculously, my car took a hard right just before the end of the bridge, sending me over four lanes of traffic. Somehow, I wasn't hit head-on or struck by another car. My car came to an abrupt stop. I immediately smelled the sulfur from my airbag and the smoke from my tires and engine. I slowly opened my eyes, unsure of what I was going to see or what I might look like. A man had pulled over and he was running toward my totaled Toyota Celica that had somehow ended up on the opposite side of the freeway. I had a burn mark on my neck from my seat belt, the left side of my head was cut, my ears were ringing, my knees were aching due to them smashing into the steering column, and my face was bleeding from my airbag going off.

I had secretly borrowed my sister's brand-new white sweatshirt to wear to work that day, and at that moment, nothing was more important to me than her shirt. The first thing I said to the guy who got to my car was, "My sister is going to kill me! Please tell me there isn't any blood on this shirt!"

"No, but I would have shaved if I knew I was going to meet such a beautiful young lady," he said. *WTF? I can't even get in a car accident without attracting a douchebag!*

"Please help me. I need you to call my dad."

"You're going to be okay. I'm going to stay with you."

"Sir, we're going to need you to step away," a paramedic said.

"Do you want me to ride with you in the ambulance?" the man asked over the paramedic's shoulder.

"Do you know this guy, ma'am?"

I shook my head no and closed my eyes, thankful to be alive.

I had worked at my dad's company the summer prior, so thankfully my best friend had the number to reach him. She called his office and told him she didn't know if I was dead or alive, but another friend from high school saw that a car like mine was totaled on the freeway and saw a blonde on a stretcher. My dad was too upset to drive to the hospital, so my grandpa drove him.

"Where's Mom?" I asked. He said he couldn't call her until he knew I was alive, and that was the first time I heard him say "I love you." It meant everything to me to hear those words from him.

After that, I saw my brother and sister. I had hoped for a hug, but that didn't happen. Neither are huggers like me, but that's okay. I held on to what really mattered, and that was my dad saying he loved me. Years later, I saw a psychic, and without me mentioning the prayer that I screamed in my car, she said a guardian angel had carried me across the traffic. I have no doubt that is true. I believe that this accident happened, not to me, but for me, to give me the gift of those three words from my dad.

IT'S NOT YOUR FAULT, BUT IT'S YOUR JOB TO HEAL IT

The topic of letting go of blame makes me think of a client I coached, Ashley*, who had been married to an alcoholic narcissist for twenty years. Even after the divorce, her energy was still beaten down from how she had been treated by her ex. It was time for her to heal the pain that was keeping her stuck, so that she could attract men who would treat her better.

Most recently, she was hitting it off with a guy, then he suddenly ended things. She was left feeling confused and, once again, feeling rejected and unworthy of receiving love.

"The guys that you're meeting now—what are they like?" I asked. She was attracting narcissistic men who were super-fit and very into their looks, just like her ex.

One guy had said to her, "You have a beautiful smile, but I don't see this working." The comment made her self-conscious about her body. Her ex had always made her feel bad and constantly criticized her body, even when she was in great shape. Having that old pattern and story reappear proved to her that her limiting belief was right, that she was not worthy of being with.

When I asked her about other times she felt the same pain of rejection because of her body or appearance, she remembered that her alcoholic father had told her she was fat when she was a teenager. She realized her ex and her dad had more in common than she thought, besides both being alcoholic narcissists.

She went through the forgiveness process, even though her dad had passed away. She became open to seeing how he was raised by an abusive alcoholic father and imagined what his upbringing must've been like. Through this process, she was able to let some things go, even though they hurt.

Understandably, if we care about fitness, we want our partner to as well, but connecting the dots for Ashley helped her see why she was attracting the same kind of men. With this awareness, she released the pain she felt from her dad's judgment and her ex-husband's abusive behavior so that she could finally begin to heal her past and break the cycle.

A universal signal, or message, goes out for whatever belief you're vibing at, and for Ashley, she had a story on repeat stemming from her childhood—that being thin was important to men, so she attracted men who would criticize her body just like her dad did when she was a teenager. Why? Because the pain of this event was still lingering.

Heal Yourself
DELETE THE OLD PROGRAMS

Just like a computer, there are programs running behind the scenes in our minds, and those programs are the stories and beliefs we tell ourselves about ourselves. Sometimes you need to hit CTRL-ALT-DEL and shut down a program that's not working for you, like Ashley did with her belief that her dad's criticism was correct, or like I did with my belief that my dad didn't love me. Those subconscious stories from childhood play a major role in the types of relationships and situations you're attracting.

Answer these reflection questions to uncover some stories relating to family dynamics that may be running in the background, stories that you might want to re-examine:

- What beliefs do you have about your parents?
- What beliefs have you carried with you from your childhood?
- What story do you have on repeat?

- What emotional wounds do you need to heal from your childhood?
- What belief are you collecting evidence on? (Clue: When do you say "See, I knew this would happen!")

Review what you've written about your upbringing and what came up for you. This is part of the healing journey. We can't change the past but we can stop letting it define our future.

CHAPTER 8

F Him

As I was writing this book, my dad called me to tell me how proud he is of me. He said, "Shorty, you're an angel if you've forgiven any of the men you dated who broke your heart."

I replied, "Well I guess I'm an angel then, because I have, and I hope I can help other women do the same so they can meet *their* Mr. Right." And that's what this chapter is about—forgiveness.

Before I go any further, I need you to know that this forgiveness didn't happen overnight. Hardly. There were five years between when I broke up with Todd and when I really started working with the therapist who helped me heal my past and realize I wasn't a victim. As he helped me see that my exes happened "for" me and not "to" me, I started appreciating what all my exes had taught me, especially Todd.

I released the guilt and shame I held about him stealing from my grandfather, and me not realizing what a con artist he was until it was too late. I replaced those feelings with gratitude that he showed me his true colors before we got married and had children. Thankfully, I dodged *those* bullets. He also showed me what kind of relationship I *don't* want to be in—a relationship based on lies and deceit, with someone smothering me or appeasing me with what they can buy or do for me. Through this process, I became aware that I couldn't hate him and be grateful for the lessons he taught me at the same time. Little by little, I was able to create space in my heart for more of what I truly desired in my life. I had to heal my inner world so that I would be able to love someone the same way I deserved to be loved.

There are two sides to forgiveness. It's not just about the other person; it's also about self-forgiveness.

Besides appreciating the wisdom in the wounds (more about this concept later in the chapter), a forgiveness exercise in a life coaching class really moved the needle for me to forgive Todd and myself. We paired up with partners and shared a bit about our story, about someone who hurt us deeply. The idea of this exercise was to imagine the person in front of you as being the person you want an apology from (an apology which may not ever happen in real life). My partner looked me straight in the eye, and with the most genuine look on his face said, "Stacey, I'm *so* sorry for what I did to you. I'm sorry for betraying you and your family and I'm sorry for any pain that I caused you or Jaide. Neither of you deserved to go through what I put you through."

I stared back at him and let the tears flow. It was powerful and extremely healing to imagine getting a sincere apology from someone who destroyed my life in a hot minute. I felt like I could trust myself again and stop holding myself responsible for his actions.

Be sure to forgive yourself for whatever you think you did or failed to do. You will do better next time.

When we lay it all out, we see it's not our burden to carry. I carried a lot of shame and guilt around for years about what Todd did. When I finally found the courage to share this story with my future husband, we had been dating for a year. He said, "You shouldn't feel ashamed. You didn't do anything wrong. He did." I was ashamed even telling him the story, for him to know this had happened in my life. I was fearful he was going to judge me, or think I had too much "baggage" for him, but he never made me feel that way. Instead, he genuinely listened, shared his insight, and helped me see that I was holding on to someone else's baggage, and it wasn't mine to carry. It was time to let it go and forgive myself.

Other people's bad choices aren't ours to own or hold on to. Those choices are theirs, and theirs alone. I share this story to give you hope that there *are* men out there who will help you heal and grow if you are open to it. I would never have seen this side of my husband if I hadn't opened up and shared this moment of vulnerability with him. Being with a man who I felt emotionally and physically safe with was a night and day shift from the douchebags I'd been with, who would throw my past in my face or use it against me down the road.

I'm continuing to practice self-forgiveness, even as I write this book. It's been years since I've had to think about the details of these stories, and to be able to share them with my husband has been healing. I shared chapters with him, and his response was, "I can't believe that you, my wife who tolerates zero bullshit and disrespect, would ever go through any of this. You're one of the strongest women I've ever met."

This story makes me think of a recent and unattributed post I saw on Instagram: **"Everyone comes with baggage. Find someone who loves you enough to help you unpack."**

THERE'S WISDOM IN THE WOUNDS
When you forgive, you're setting yourself free, not forgetting what he did or letting him off the hook.

The more forgiveness work I did, discovering the purpose in the pain, the more it allowed me to see the situation with Todd differently, and instead be grateful for the lessons he taught me, even though it was years later. I started thinking, *Thank you for showing me how important it is to forgive others and myself. Thank you for showing me what I needed to improve on in my life. Thank you for giving me an opportunity to show Jaide what it looks like to be a strong woman.*

That gratitude was part of my forgiveness journey—forgiving him and forgiving myself. It's very powerful to get to a place where you can look at your heartache and see what you gained from the experience, not just what you lost.

What if you can forgive yourself and your ex? You're probably thinking something my clients often say when we get to the forgiveness part: "Excuse me? He doesn't deserve my forgiveness." You're right. He probably doesn't deserve it, but *you* deserve to feel free from this heavy emotion.

If you're not ready or if it's too soon, that's okay too. This is your journey, so honor where you are on your path. If anything, finish this book and then come back when you're ready to implement the simple steps I'm going to teach you, steps that could help move you closer to living a life beyond your wildest dreams.

This part may seem extremely uncomfortable, and you may want to shut the book and/or never read another one of my books again. I get it. Believe it or not, the resistance you may be feeling is a great sign that you're on the right path to healing your heart. Your ego is telling you it's not safe to forgive, or that this is going to be too hard. I've been there.

Consider how I just went from one dysfunctional relationship to the next because I didn't take the time to heal or get closure. I thought forgiveness was a sign of weakness, or that these men would somehow win if I forgave them. Boy, was I wrong! Forgiving myself and my exes granted me the emotional freedom I dreamed about for years. If I hadn't done that, those exes would still be taking up prime real estate in my heart, and I wouldn't have had any room for someone new, especially someone emotionally available like my husband.

Remember, I had a guy con $80,000 from my dying grandfather. For years, I thought I could never forgive him, but I did. Why? Because I wanted to live my best life and I was hell-bent on showing up as the best version of myself for my daughter. I didn't want to carry around anger and hate in my heart for another human being.

RELEASE WHAT'S NOT YOURS

My client Arianna* came to me saying things like, "All men are liars," "Men just hurt you and leave," and "You can never trust a man, so it doesn't matter." She was saying these general ideas as if they were absolutely true, so I asked her where she learned this mindset from.

Her story went back to when she was five years old, when her dad had an affair and left her mom. She was stuck at home alone a lot and felt like her parents were more concerned with hating each other than with loving her and making sure she felt safe in the situation. As an adult, she still felt like that little girl looking out the window, wishing she wasn't alone. Those statements about men were her own opinions based on her dad's behavior, and also things her mom said all the time, so she took them to be true. She lived by those words, and unfortunately spent years attracting the exact thing she didn't want—a marriage like the one her parents had.

Here's how I helped her give those stories back to her mom and dad:

1. I asked her to take all those details—about her dad having an affair and leaving, her mom's beliefs about men and relationships, how their divorce made her feel, all the badmouthing of each other, etc.—and put them in a beautiful box, metaphorically. One box for each parent.
2. Wrap each box up with a beautiful bow.
3. Imagine yourself giving these gifts to your mom and dad.
4. Then, picture them standing there, each with their box. Let them deal with their choices.

Using this exercise, Arianna was able to forgive her parents and let go of the resentment, anger, and sadness that she had been holding on to for so long. This allowed her to create new empowering beliefs, which eventually led to her attracting better relationships.

I was able to give Todd's actions back to him with this "put it in the box" exercise too. If a man has broken your heart, do this exercise, before entering another relationship if possible. If I had done this exercise after each of my relationships, especially after Nick, maybe I wouldn't have been such an energetic match for the next cheater.

Give this a try: I want you to close your eyes and think about all the things that make you angry about your ex. How things ended. All the pain. All the lies. All the arguments. All the stories he told you that aren't yours to sort through. Anything that is upsetting you right now or that you think about often. Now, imagine putting all of that in a box, tying a beautiful bow around it, and walking up to him, standing tall, and handing it back to him with a smile, saying, "Here you go, this is your shit to carry around, not mine." Watch this person take the box and you can then turn around and walk away.

The point of this exercise is to help you see that his treatment of you is about him and the emotional baggage that he brought into the relationship—baggage that he needs to deal with. It's not yours to carry around or bring with you into your next relationship. You have your own "box" to unload and to worry about; you don't need his too.

Think about what happens if you don't do this forgiveness work. Imagine that we each have luggage that we carry with us from relationship to relationship, and the suitcase keeps getting heavier with each breakup. This is why it's important to take the time to heal and to unpack your emotional baggage if you truly want to attract and keep a healthy relationship.

CREATE SPACE FOR MR. RIGHT

When I teach forgiveness work, my focus is on trying to help my client heal their heart and create space for the relationship they truly desire. It's hard to create a future that includes everything you want when you're holding on to old pain and carrying around all this emotional baggage. You must let go of the old to create space for the new.

As you unpack the emotional baggage and clear the clutter from your past, you also create space for new possibilities and healthier relationships. That's why we can't skip the forgiveness process and the "clear the clutter" step. As I shared in Chapter 1, *Radical Forgiveness* put me on my spiritual path to understanding why things were happening for me and not to me. I began to see my life through different lenses, which gave me the courage to begin to let the past go. I didn't realize it at the time, but it helped me attract my husband into my life.

Let's "Marie Kondo" your past. That means we're going to clear out all the things that do not spark joy and what is energetically blocking you from living your best life. Old stuff carries old energy, and what you focus on expands, so by decluttering items from your past you let the universe know that you are ready to let go of the old to make room for the new.

So, get rid of, repurpose, or donate any of your ex's stuff that you're hanging on to, or any of your clothes or underwear (okay, maybe don't donate your underwear, but you get the idea) that remind you of them. This includes bed sheets, pictures, text messages, social media posts, even the wine opener he brought to your place and never took back. Even if it's shoved in the back of a drawer, that thing is still holding on to the memory of your ex. This especially goes for any jewelry he gave you. There's still an energetic connection between the two of you, so the universe is confused on what you want—you're hoping to find true love, but still holding on to items from a man who broke your heart. So, let's set the intention to clear out that box of goodies and items— their only job is to upset you.

Let's start with that box of letters and pictures you've been holding on to that's shoved in the corner of your closet or hidden in the garage. It's time to go through the box and clear out old memories that don't bring you joy. Trust me, you'll feel so much lighter. If you're not ready to toss these items, that's okay, but this would be a great time to ask yourself why you feel that way. What are you still holding on to? Is it what could have been? Or how great it was at the beginning? I get it. It wasn't easy for me to go through stacks of old pictures from vacations, holidays, or outings with friends, but I was ready to fully move on from these men, which meant it was time to bless and release these items. I thanked the person in the picture for guiding me to where I am today and then put each picture through my shredder.

The day came when it was time for me to let go of my wedding dress and the engagement ring from Todd. I knew it would help my heart heal if the items went to a good home. I decided to donate my beautiful beaded wedding dress and matching accessories to an organization that benefited brides who were breast cancer survivors and who didn't have the funds to pay for a wedding dress.

My engagement ring was a different story. I didn't want to just *give* it away, but I knew being greedy wasn't going to help me move forward in my healing process. I asked my angels to guide me in the process, for the highest good of all. I received an intuitive hit to list the ring on Craigslist. I immediately thought of all the crime stories you hear of people getting mugged, but lucky for me, the people I heard from asked to meet in public. The first stop was at a high-end jewelry store that basically offered me two gumballs for it. I reminded the jeweler of the paperwork I held in my hand that showed the original price, but he held firm. I respectfully declined and left. Next, I received a call from a gentleman who said he was interested in the ring to replace his wife's wedding ring, which she had lost while drunk at a concert. *Next.* My last stop was to meet a man at a jewelry store at the mall. He asked that his jeweler check the stone out to make sure it was legit, which it was.

"Why is this ring available?" the potential buyer asked.

"It was best that I didn't follow through with the wedding, but I hope it brings joy to the person I end up selling it to," I said. He looked surprised at my answer, then shared that he had little money when he and his wife got married, but now that times were different, he wanted to surprise his wife with an upgraded ring for their twentieth wedding anniversary. *Sold.* After the transaction was done, his wife hugged me with tears in her eyes. She told me she was sorry to hear that my wedding didn't happen, but she wanted me to know how much she appreciates and loves her beautiful new ring.

Removing physical clutter and making room for what you want increases the universe's clarity about what you are an energetic match for.

Heal Yourself
FORGIVENESS CHECKLIST

Let's start with you and forgiveness in general. Here are some questions to check in with yourself on where you are now when it comes to the idea of forgiveness:

- Do you forgive often, or do you hold on to old pain, hoping it will somehow make the other person feel horrible? If you're stuck in a pattern of not forgiving yourself or refusing to forgive others, there's no room for something or someone better to come into your life.
- Do you constantly talk shit about your ex? If so, don't you think he's gotten enough airtime by now? The more you heal your heart, the less you'll want to talk about him.
- Do you badmouth your family members or friends behind their backs? If so, this may be a sign you need to do this work.
- Do you find that you're angry more often than happy? We all have bad days, but if you're walking around like a bull in a china shop, that is no way to attract the love of your life or bring in more abundance.

As you continue to examine your resistance and find ways to shift it, you'll feel that negative energy release its hold on you. The next exercise will help you work on that by shifting the words you use to talk about yourself and what happened in the past.

WORDS CARRY ENERGY

If you have a story on repeat, one that you tell over and over again about how someone broke your heart, then you're amplifying that negative energy and creating more emotional clutter that is blocking the man of your dreams from finding you. Yes, it is important to talk about what happened, but not for years after the event—and not to every single person you come in contact with. One way to stop the momentum of this negative energy is to find the wisdom in your wounds so that you can rewrite those stories as a douchebag survivor, not a victim.

Identify the breakup story that you continue to tell or obsess over, then go through the questions below to discover the wisdom in those wounds:

- What did he teach you about yourself?
- Did he teach you how strong you are and that you can get through a heartbreak?
- Did he teach you that you need to focus on loving yourself more?
- Did he teach you that you may need stronger boundaries?
- Did he show you what you're not willing to put up with in a relationship?
- Did he show you what you don't want in a relationship?
- Did he show you what you *do* want in a relationship?

Great! Write it all down. This will help you identify where you are now on your healing journey.

THANK YOU FOR SHOWING ME

Now that you've discovered what it is you needed to learn, the next step is to bring in the "Thank You for Showing Me" method. Fill in these blanks using your answers from the above section.

"Thank you, (insert name, or "asshole" is fine too), for showing me (insert what he taught you)!

Give each affirmation a voice by saying them out loud. You now have a new empowering story to tell.

The next time you want to share your story, just be sure to end it in a positive way. For example, I became aware of how often I was telling my low-vibe Todd story. After doing this exercise, I noticed I was sharing the story less often, but when I did, I also shared the lessons I learned, how grateful I was for each of them, and how I used the experience to improve my life. Nine times out of ten, the listener would tell me that I'd found a great way of looking at my heartbreak, and share her own story of heartbreak. Then, I would help her find the lessons. This is how my coaching business started to blossom. My hope is that, as you start sharing your story this way, you can help other women find their empowering story too.

Finding wisdom in the wounds is a surefire way to quickly shift your energy and transform your life. This is a great tool to use in any situation in which you feel wronged. You'll be able to pair your new story about the past with the next exercise, which will help you isolate your thoughts so that they don't control your actions.

BECOME AWARE OF YOUR THOUGHTS

Your mindset, how you view dating, and what you tell yourself all play a part in what type of man you attract into your life. So, it's important to clear out any limiting beliefs that are preventing you from attracting Mr. Right. Answer these questions to uncover those old beliefs that the new you, who's forgiving herself and others, won't hold as true anymore:

- What lies are you telling yourself about finding love?
- Do you say you want to be in love but then you don't actually take any steps toward falling in love?
- Do you tell yourself you don't have time to date, or that you'd rather be single? Think about how much time you spend mindlessly scrolling through social media feeds, or binge-watching TV. You have plenty of time to date.
- Have you convinced yourself that there are no good guys left? Well, there are seven billion people in the world. There are plenty of good men left, but you need to get out there to meet them.
- Do you tell yourself that you'll get back into dating after you lose weight, but then you find yourself not going to the gym or eating healthy? Of course you do! You're keeping yourself safe. Instead, be honest with yourself. If you

really don't want to get out there, then don't. I wouldn't be surprised though, that when you change this narrative you will go to the gym, eat healthy, lose weight, and meet a great man.

- Do you tell yourself that love isn't safe? Love is safe, and it's what we all desire. The unhealed emotions that you're carrying around from your past are what don't feel safe.
- Do you constantly complain to your friends about how much you hate dating, but then wonder why dating sucks? Get honest with yourself about which part of dating you despise—this is the area that needs some work. Dating should be fun! If it's not, figure out which part you're uncomfortable with and tweak it.

These can be uncomfortable questions to answer, but they are crucial to helping you become empowered and love yourself to such a degree that you're emotionally available for a kind and caring guy.

Now you're ready to have more happy dates!

CHAPTER 9

Have More Happy Dates

"Oh, is he too nice to you?" my friend jokingly asked about my date. The guy had a great job and was super good-looking, but I just didn't feel like there was a special connection.

I was in a vicious cycle of my own expectations—I expected men to be disrespectful and leave me with a broken heart. This cycle began when I was a teenager and continued until I hit rock bottom at age thirty-five. When I met a nice guy, I had no idea what to do with him, so I would find myself making up excuses as to why it wouldn't work between us.

I was recently telling this story to a friend, and she said she used to do the same thing.

For example, she went on a date with a guy, and everything was perfect. They had dinner and walked on the beach. He kissed her, and then brought her home at a reasonable hour. He was a store manager working on his MBA. However, unlike her, he had a great relationship with both his parents and wasn't frustrated with school or life. She felt like they had nothing in common because she was a hot mess. When she did manage to be asked on a date by a gentleman, she would sabotage it.

As we unpacked her story, I noticed similarities between her and myself. Back then, when I sabotaged my dates, I had a belief that I wasn't aware of until I started doing this work. It was that, deep down, I believed I was unworthy of love and respect. So, when a guy would show me genuine respect or show any signs he was falling in love with me, I would run for the hills. It just didn't feel right to me, because we weren't on the same energetic playing field. I'd either pick the guy apart and find everything "wrong" with him, or I'd think he was boring. I was so used to having drama attached to relationships that when it wasn't there, I'd lose interest.

Most women don't flat out say they want a bad boy so they can get their hearts stomped on—but we gravitate toward that "bad boy" type anyway. Why? Because, in a messed up way, it becomes our normal. The energy feels familiar, and if it's not there, we unconsciously create the drama we're used to. That energy and history repeats itself until we intentionally shift our energy and consciously make the choice to create a new normal.

I knew I needed to create a new normal, so I started by increasing my sense of worthiness and self-love. If I want to be loved, I need to love myself. If I want respect, I need to respect myself. I also needed to drop the codependency act and discover how to become whole and complete without a man in my life.

In this chapter, I'm going to tell you about a few other women I've coached who were stuck in a similar rut and how I helped them discover what was really underneath their dating fails.

BE OPEN TO RECEIVE

"I hate everything about dating, especially when a guy wants to pay the bill," my client Reese* told me. She was so uncomfortable on dates that she would spend most of the time wondering if the guy was having a good time, and the rest of the time dreading the arrival of the check.

"That sounds stressful. Tell me about some of the guys you're meeting," I said. Reese actually reminded me a lot of myself in my twenties. She was also climbing the corporate ladder and looking for love in all the wrong places. For her, that meant wasting time scrolling through a dating app for the hottest shirtless guy.

She went on to tell me that she would text her girlfriends after the date to let them know the guy was awesome, but the next day she'd regret she ever said that and wonder why she thought the date was so great. She would spend the day self-sabotaging, thinking about how he wasn't really her type, and eventually ghost him. This cycle would prove her deep-rooted belief that she should indeed "not be dating" right, time and time again. It would also confirm once again why she hated everything about dating. It was a vicious cycle.

I needed to explore more about why she was so bothered about men paying for her. I had a feeling it was deeper than her just not wanting a man to take care of her, but I had to ask.

"Why do you dread when the bill comes?"

She told me that her ex-boyfriend had expected her to pay for everything, then he'd disappear and only come back into her life when he needed money.

"Why did you keep paying for him?" I asked.

"That was the only time he appreciated me," she said.

"How do you know that?" I asked.

It turned out that, as a little girl, Reese watched her mom give her dad whatever he wanted, all the time, even after their divorce. He never paid child support or alimony, and only came around when he wanted something—usually money or sex. If he didn't want something from her mom, he was out of there. So, she felt like the only way to keep a guy around was to pay for him, and that guys just wanted to use her.

Flash forward to why her dates with men who wanted to take care of the check were so traumatizing. On her dates, when the guy reached for the check, she felt guilty that he was paying for her—like if she can't give him money, she won't have any value in his eyes. So, in a twisted way, when guys paid the tab, she didn't feel that they were trying to take care of her—she felt like they didn't need her. She couldn't see it as the man taking care of her because she didn't believe she was *worthy* of a man taking care of her, because her dad didn't.

I helped her see how the story she learned as a child, the story of her feelings of unworthiness and the link to men's behavior, was determining her experience on these dates when the check came. She agreed to start recognizing when she becomes triggered and then ask herself the following questions: "Is this something that I learned in my childhood? When have I felt like this before? Is this stemming from something my ex said to me?"

She also learned in our session that her lack of self-worth was showing up in the form of therapy shopping, when she'd spend thousands of dollars on herself and rack up credit card debt. She didn't even wear a lot of the things she bought, but shopping was her way of trying to fill that void of her dad not providing for her. She was also caught up in counting the number of "likes" she was getting on social media. A post that got crickets would make her feel like that ignored kid again.

We figured out that she was using shopping and social media to find the validation that she lacked in her childhood. I suggested that the next time Reese wanted to feel fulfilled—now that she was aware of her shopping addiction—she should spend time with herself, and even write herself a love note, or do something else that would make her feel valued and loved. We decided it was also time to take a break from the dating app and social media. I suggested that instead, she might spend her free time working on loving herself so she can become her own biggest fan, because she is deserving of a man taking care of her.

Feeling like you're of value isn't always about spending money or how many followers you have. Reese began to see her true beauty instead of trying to buy those feelings of approval or focusing on how many friends acknowledged her on social media.

NO MORE GHOSTING

> Change the way you look at things, and
> the things you look at change.
> - Wayne Dyer

I worked with a woman, Emily*, a young professional who was trying to meet men on a dating app. She told me she wasn't having trouble meeting good men, but rather she struggled with keeping them. She was stuck in a cycle. First, she'd finally get back on the dating app after convincing herself that's what she "should" be doing. Then, she would meet a great guy who checked all of the boxes, they would talk every day for a week, make plans to get together, and then he would either ghost her or cancel at the last minute.

"Why do you feel you 'should' be on a dating app?" I asked.

"I'm not getting any younger, and my mom is concerned my clock is running out."

"What part of dating do you not enjoy?" I asked.

"All of it. I hate small talk, like I get hives just thinking about it—and my time and personal space are what I view as most valuable to me. And I like being single," she said.

"Okay, all valid points. Tell me more about your last serious relationship."

"He broke things off out of the blue, and I haven't spoken to him since."

Now we're getting somewhere, I thought.

As we continued to chat and unravel her story, it became clear that Emily had not gotten over an ex from seven years ago. The relationship hadn't ended on her terms, which created in her a belief that love isn't safe and being in a relationship only means one thing—rejection. She thought she was ready to find love again, but realized she had some blocks that she needed to work through and old pain to process.

She was still holding space for a relationship that no longer existed and kept dreaming of what could have been. With her doing this, there just wasn't room for a new man to come into her life.

Although she claimed she was ready to meet someone, she needed to be honest with herself. The message her energy was sending out to the universe was that she was still in love with her ex, and every guy who ghosted her or canceled at the last minute clearly received that universal message too. She could see the connection and agreed that it was time to forgive her ex and release him.

We didn't get there overnight. The first step was for her to be aware that she was repelling men. Next, she had to acknowledge why that was happening, and then let go of the old relationship. She admitted that she had been stuck in this story of blaming him for her unhappiness and it felt safer to stay single. She missed who she used to be and had lost herself after the breakup, so she agreed that she needed to practice self-love and have more fun.

There was also an aspect of forgiveness work to the process. With the awareness that she was attracting men who were proving her limiting beliefs (like that it wasn't safe to be in love and was safer to be single) she could forgive herself for not knowing better. Emily was able to see the wisdom in the wounds and understand how important it is to heal your heart before getting back in the saddle and trying to date again. This simple exercise elevated her emotional state from feeling discouraged to feeling grateful.

It wasn't long after that point that Emily reported back that the ghosting had stopped, and she was enjoying dating again. Because she took on the forgiveness work, she was able to release her past and shift the direction of her love life.

CHANGE THE GAME, DON'T HATE THE PLAYERS

A lot of the time, the men who break our hearts aren't committing crimes or lying to our faces…but sometimes they are. In order to meet guys who would be open to a real, honest, and loving relationship, we have to look at where we might not be real, honest, or loving toward ourselves. That's how to break the vicious cycle and release the negative energy that wreaks havoc on our relationships.

The same principle applies if you're frustrated with the men you're finding through dating apps or out on the town. Change your expectations and beliefs to change your outcomes.

Imagine what might shift if you approach dating with an open heart and an expectation that you're going to meet a good guy, or have a good time on the date, and delete the guys who are showing you red flags. Rejecting what you don't want also signals to the universe what you do want.

As I explained with Reese's story, you can interrupt your pattern the next time you get triggered by being aware of the cycle you're in. Then, you can make different choices using that observation. Reese realized her reaction was tied to what she learned as a child and then, with that knowledge, opted not to bring that baggage with her on her future dates. If she hadn't identified her pattern, she probably would have continued to be uncomfortable when men paid on dates, or even worse, she might have met another guy who would use her for her money. Staying in the same pattern will keep getting you the same results.

When we heal our hearts from past pain, it's less likely that the same issue will continue to reappear and sabotage us in the future. Emily need-ed to heal her wounded heart and clear the clutter of that ex who was long gone. Reese's challenge was to become more loving and accepting of herself. It's important to remove old patterns so that you're able to be open to receive a new reality for your life. And, when you show up dif-ferently, you invite new and exciting changes in what's possible for you.

Heal Yourself
HAPPY DATE MINDSET CHECKLIST

I created this checklist so that when you're not going on dates or meet-ing the man of your dreams, you can identify what inner work to focus on to change who you're attracting:

- Do you tell yourself you're never going to meet a good guy? If so, start to pay attention to how often you tell yourself that.
- What do you believe to be true about yourself? (You're not like the other women who have found love, etc.)
- Do you see a happy couple and think, "Are they REALLY that happy?"

- Do you tell yourself that you're happier being single, or that you're too busy to date?
- What about self-love? Are you wearing a bra that's so old you can see through it? And when was the last time you got new underwear? What's your bedroom like? Is it a cluster-fuck, or does it feel inviting? If you want sexy to show up in your life, then you need to *feel* sexy.

Use this checklist to gain clarity and to clear out beliefs that no longer serve you. Being in a low-vibe mindset restricts the good-feeling vibe of love. That is not where you'll attract Mr. Right. The lower vibrations are where the men who are low-vibe reside because their job is to show you—it's time to rise, girl!

DATING CHECK-IN

Decide how much time is too much time to spend on figuring out whether or not to move forward in the relationship. Give yourself a deadline and ask yourself the following questions:

- How do I feel when I'm around him?
- Does he talk to me with respect?
- Can I be my authentic self, or do I feel I need to act a certain way when he's around?
- Is he meeting my emotional needs?
- How's the communication?
- What do I enjoy about him? What do I *not* enjoy about him?
- Have I noticed any red flags?
- Am I feeling a connection with him, or am I trying to make it work?

Avoid self-doubt and only accept men you feel are a good match for you.

CHAPTER 10

The Universe Loves Clarity

The August after I met Jeff, I returned to the same work event where I'd first met him the year before. This time, however, I was armed with my new therapist's approach and deep inner work, so I showed up differently. Someone else showed up differently, too. The coworker that tended to be quiet and keep to himself was standing around laughing, joking, and looking as handsome as ever—which got my attention.

"Hi Chris," I said with a flirty smile.

"Hey, Stacey! Good to see you. It's been a while," he replied.

"Yeah, I think the last time I saw you, you were feeling no pain," I teased.

He chuckled. "Yeah, last year was pretty rough, but things are better now."

We already have something in common, I thought.

A bunch of us went out after the event, and this time I wasn't interested in anyone who wasn't a good fit for me. I had my eye on Chris, but had to play it cool and sit at another table.

"Do these condiment bottles ever get wiped down?" I muttered as I cleaned them off with the disinfectant wipes I had in my purse.

"What are you, a germaphobe?" Chris yelled over to the table.

"Yep! You have a problem with that?" I joked back.

"Not at all!" he smiled.

Chris was hanging out with Adam*, a guy who I knew to be a player at work, so I was on guard and aware that Chris could be the same type. We all decided to ditch the dive bar and go to a nearby club in downtown Seattle, which was more my style. Chris asked if he and Adam could get a ride with me to the club. We piled into my car, and I went to put my seatbelt on—only to find a dirty mustard bottle in the pocket of my black leather jacket.

"Gross!" I laughed, as I tossed the bottle to him in the back seat. He definitely had an interesting way of flirting, but he made me laugh, so I went with it.

At the next place, I bee-lined it to the bathroom, praying it would be cleaner than the last place. Chris and Adam headed straight for the bar. I noticed Chris talking to a girl with Adam and I didn't want to interrupt, so I took a hard left and found the rest of the group.

But Chris had gotten my attention, and of course, I knew where he worked. The following Monday, I taped my business card to the mustard bottle and wrote: "You forgot me :)" on the back. I packaged it up and asked my assistant if she would get it shipped to Chris Dewald right away. Not knowing what it was, she responded, "Absolutely! I'll get it shipped out this afternoon."

A few days later I received a playful email from Chris saying, "Good one!" This was the start of something different.

I had gotten better at being alone, and as I got to know myself, I knew I could find someone who appreciated me and my humor. I was being honest with myself, the people around me, and my counselor, as opposed to pushing away any offer of help. I became open to receiving and having more fun. That was a big part of Chris showing up, that I had strengthened my ability to create a healthy relationship with him.

We spent the next couple of months corresponding via text messaging since he lived in another state. It would have been nice if he lived closer, but I was on a mission to better my life. Having a cutie like him living near me would have slowed down my healing process. Instead, I spent time processing every emotional trigger that came up. The trigger that came up most often for me was the feeling of being alone, but I knew I needed to go through this. I needed to understand why I felt alone and why I wasn't happy just being with myself. I needed to understand why I always had to surround myself with people in order to feel content. I needed to learn how to love my own company so that someone else could too. I needed to heal the parts of me that I had been running from for years. I needed to become my own best friend.

This work helped me get to know who I was on a deeper level and who I no longer wanted to be. I would have been doing Chris a disservice if he was by my side at this time in our relationship. I had the tools to process my past and to do the inner work to create the loving relationship I wanted, but I knew the loving relationship that I craved needed to begin with me. I was the only person who could change my life.

This is when I began studying the Law of Attraction, read *Radical Forgiveness,* and started listening to Abraham Hicks's *Ask and It Is Given,* on my long commute to and from work, instead of being on the phone, listening to my friends' drama. It's not that I didn't care, but I had enough drama of my own to deal with.

Finally, in late September, Chris got up the guts to ask me out. He was driving up from Portland to Seattle. I have never been so freaking nervous for a date in my entire life.

Chris wasn't familiar with downtown Seattle, so I offered to pick him up from his hotel. We started at Twist, a swanky bar in Belltown.

Little did I know that October 1, 2010, would be the start of a beautiful new relationship.

I'll never forget the feeling of knowing, without a shadow of a doubt, that Chris was the one—and it all started with our first hug. It felt so safe, and was an embrace like I had never experienced. I looked up to the sky during our hug and quietly said "Thank you." It felt as if he had been sent from above.

Instead of sabotaging this new healthy relationship, I welcomed it by working on opening my heart and affirming that I deserved to receive it. My relationship with Chris felt easy; everything was transparent and it never felt like there was drama between us. He taught me how to love openly and what a healthy relationship looks like.

EVERYTHING WAS DIFFERENT

We started a long-distance relationship since he was in Portland and I was in Seattle. And so, for the first time in my life, I was dating a guy who didn't ghost me, or constantly change or cancel our plans. Simply put, he wasn't a douche.

Chris's marriage of twelve years had ended the previous summer, which explained why I sensed something was seriously wrong when I saw him at the work event a year prior. He was honest with me about his marriage and why it failed, which was a mirror in that I was being honest in how I was showing up. Just like the douchebags were showing me what I need to heal, Chris was showing me how far I'd come with my healing.

We didn't say "I love you" until the three-month mark, and didn't meet each other's kids until we had been together for five months. We both agreed that it was best to take it slow and not rush things.

The biggest revelation, though, was this: I didn't need him to say that he loved me to feel secure in the relationship. I was working on loving myself and focused on not looking for validation outside of myself.

It felt good to not have that stress around Chris telling me he loved me. His actions were speaking louder than his words. I'd never been in a relationship where I could *feel* how much my partner loved me without him saying a word. It was new to me, not needing a man to tell me he loved me in order to feel safe in a relationship. Nick told me he loved me all the time, and you know how that relationship went, so it was a nice change to be with a man who made sure he knew he loved me before he said it. Men should show you they love you, not just tell you.

I felt safe to grow with him, and he never once threw my past in my face, unlike other men I've dated.

We also negotiated our relationship on our own terms. I was honest about not wanting to move to Portland, Oregon, because I knew I wouldn't be happy, and I didn't want Jaide to change school districts as she entered junior high. If I hadn't done the work of really getting to know myself, I would've packed my things and relocated for all the wrong reasons, then been miserable and resented him. That wouldn't have been fair to anyone involved.

"If we need to see each other long distance until Jaide graduates, okay, but I can't relocate her," I told Chris. He agreed.

We stuck to this plan for the next two and a half years, going back and forth between states. Then, Chris decided to move to Seattle, but I didn't make the decision for him or give him an ultimatum. And honestly, it was awesome that Chris and I lived so far apart in the beginning. We had to learn how to communicate first, versus having our relationship be built on our physical attraction, which can be confusing because great sex doesn't always mean a great relationship. (Although great relationships should have great sex, great sex alone does not make for a great relationship.)

When you go for a job interview at a company, you should interview the company as well, to make sure it's a good fit for you. That's what dating should be like. Instead of worrying about whether *you're* good enough for *him*, figure out if *he* is good enough for *you*! It's good to have your guard up and know what you want, even if you think you might've found an awesome guy. It takes practice to let go of your past and to heal the old wounds.

When we first started dating, we were at Chris's house, and I found an elastic hairband on the floor next to his nightstand. Within seconds, I had an entire story created to explain how it got there. Instead, I took a deep breath, and I presented the evidence in my hand to Chris and said with my head lowered, "I'm having a moment."

"What's up?" he asked. Not looking him in the eyes, I handed him the mysterious hairband.

"You found a hairband?" I looked up to see a look of confusion on his face, then a dawning realization.

"Sweetie, I'm not your ex. That's my daughter's. She lives here, you know," he said as he pulled my chin up. That was my phrase, "having a moment," for when I was triggered in the relationship and needed to emotionally unpack my baggage. He would help me be present in those times and get through them, which was amazing and not something I was used to. There was no defensiveness or dismissing my emotions. He didn't always understand my triggers or the extent of the emotional pain that I was processing, but he knew it ran deep. He always made a point to show me I was worthy of being seen and heard, which was a reflection of how I was seeing and hearing myself for the first time. He was my person.

I want to make sure you understand that when I found the hairband, I didn't let the story that I made up in my head get the best of me. I stopped the crazy train, went straight to the source, and just asked. Here's the deal: If you're in a relationship with a man and don't feel like you can bring something up with him, that's a problem. It's not weird to ask about things when you do it from a place of genuinely wanting to know. Questioning him is a different story, though. Trust me, there were many times when I didn't take a deep breath and let the crazy train take over, resulting in Chris standing there staring at me, not knowing how to respond, and leaving me looking batshit crazy. I found myself accusing him of something before I even knew the whole story. I had to break the cycle of jumping to conclusions. Not all men are cheaters and pathological liars, and it took me a while to figure that out and internalize it. When there's nothing to hide, he'll just tell you what's going on.

The same goes for you. If your partner asks you something, don't get defensive. We all have a story, and relationships are really good at bringing up old pain. If you're not asking tough questions though, ask yourself why that is. Is it because you don't want to know the answers? It can also be confusing if there's sexual chemistry but no real emotional bonding. You may start ignoring red flags and stop paying attention to what you truly want in a relationship.

Taking things slowly made all the difference for me, and allowed me to confirm he was "the one." I continued to do the work on myself and, at the same time, let him show himself to me. I'm a firm believer that actions speak louder than words.

One thing I got clarity on with my new therapist is that I wanted a guy who adored and appreciated his mother and treated her well. The way a guy treats his mom, talks to her, and talks about her is probably going to be how he treats and speaks to and about you. I was overjoyed that Chris had a great relationship with his mom—there is so much love and respect there. Every time we visited her they had the most adorable rapport: "Is that my son?" she would ask.

And he would respond, "Is that my Mommy?" and then offer her one of his amazing hugs. Chris would do anything his mom asked of him, and did things he thought of that he knew she'd appreciate. This was a stark contrast from my exes, who treated their moms condescendingly, tried to avoid doing things for them, and talked down about them behind their backs. And it wasn't just his mom Chris respected. He only spoke kindly about his ex-wife and didn't bash her. "It's unfortunate what happened, but both of us are happier now," he'd say.

The old version of me would have gotten jealous that he had a civil relationship with his ex-wife, but the new version of me focused on what was important—that they were doing what was best for their daughter. All of this showed me what kind of man he truly was.

I also had to step back and give Chris a chance to take care of me. It wasn't easy, because I had been programmed to do everything on my own for so long. In understanding the giving and receiving of energy, I had to learn to be open to receive a compliment and be open to receive his support. I was so used to thinking, "I'll just do it myself!" or "Of course I have to take care of it!" Now it was time to check myself and be okay with him wanting to give me a hand. I used to think that if I let a man help me I was in some way weak, or that he would think I needed him. Chris helped me realize that he wanted to do nice things for me because it was his way of showing me that he genuinely cared.

It's also interesting to note that Todd had done things for me, down to putting toothpaste on my toothbrush, but let's be honest—that behavior was just plain creepy. Chris helps me with things he sees me doing for myself around the house, or errands that need to be run, and to receive that help from him, I had to believe that I deserved it and it was okay to receive it. This took a lot of practice for me.

By the time Chris's house was sold in Portland and he had moved into my home, we had been married for three months and had to learn to adapt to each other. He'd want to hug me every time I walked by, and I would wonder when the garbage was going to be taken out. Then, we did the love languages assessment from www.5lovelanguages.com, which I highly recommend. It made all the difference. Simply put, love languages are our personal ways that we show and receive love. Chris's love language was physical touch. So, I understood that if I didn't hug my guy, then I wasn't speaking his love language. My love language is acts of service. Bingo! So, the way Chris could show me he loved me was doing things like taking out the garbage or emptying the dishwasher without me asking. Knowing our love languages from the beginning has saved us from many arguments. Be curious about who you are, who your mate is, and what you both need to be fulfilled in the relationship.

Heal Yourself
RADIATE THE LOVE YOU WANT TO RECEIVE

Your energy flows where your attention goes. In other words, what you focus on expands, so focus on what you DO want, not on what you DON'T want. With that in mind, let's start obsessing over your ideal guy, not about the douchebags.

In order for your Mr. Right to find you—yes, find *you*, because you're going to be too busy working on loving yourself and having fun to be looking for him—you need to get crystal clear on what you truly desire in a mate. If not, the universe will continue to send you men who aren't a good match.

To make it easier, here are some questions to help you gain clarity on what you want in your Mr. Right—not what you're used to having, or what you had before, but what you are deciding now that you choose for yourself:

- Does he enjoy working out?
- Does he have good eating habits?
- Does he clean up after himself?
- Does he live on his own?
- Does he help clean the house?
- What's his relationship like with his family?
- If you're a parent, what would his relationship be like with your children?
- What are his friends like?
- Is he romantic?
- Does he remember special dates?
- Does he leave you random love notes?
- Is he spiritual?
- Is he part of a religion?
- What are his political views?
- Is he open to personal development?
- Does he enjoy traveling?
- Is he spontaneous?
- Does he enjoy the outdoors?
- What does he like to do for fun?
- Does he have a good work ethic?
- Does he have career goals?
- Is he good with money?
- What are his morals and values? Do they match yours? (If you don't know what your morals and values are,

you'll more than likely tend to attract men who don't have morals or values themselves. The more clarity you have about who YOU are, the better chance you'll attract the same.)

As a bonus, remind yourself of what DID work in your past relationships that you want more of and add those things in as well. Also consider what you didn't like about your ex—if your ex was selfish in bed, describe your Mr. Right as a giver (see how your selfish ex showed you what you DO want in life?).

NON-NEGOTIABLES

Non-negotiables are a great way to weed out the douchebags and stop wasting your valuable time. Having these clear boundaries for yourself will help you stay focused, no matter how hot the guy is.

As you describe what you want in your man, you'll also find yourself coming up with non-negotiables, or "must-haves."

Here are a few examples to get you started:

- If you're a highly educated and successful woman, your non-negotiable may be:
  - My man must have a college degree and be driven to succeed in his career.
- If you're a very fit woman (and assuming eating healthy is important to you), your non-negotiable may be:
  - My man must take care of himself and have a healthy diet.
- If you're a woman who knows that you do want children, your non-negotiable may be:
  - My man must want children.
- If you're a single mother, your non-negotiable may be:
  - My man must be open to being a step-parent one day.
- If you're living a sober life, your non-negotiable may be:
  - My man must respect that I am sober or be sober himself.

If you're having trouble coming up with a few, think back to what you tolerated in your past relationships, things you couldn't imagine tolerating now.

The Mr. Right Order exercise later in the book and deciding on your non-negotiables will both help you gain clarity on who you are and what you want to attract into your romantic relationships. And work in your love language insights, too. If you know that your main love language is receiving gifts, be sure to add that Mr. Right will love to surprise you with gifts. If quality time is your main love language, then place your order for a man who is going to love staying in and watching a movie with you on a Friday night instead of going out.

This information will help your future partner know what is important to you as well and help you place your order for Mr. Right, sending the douchebags packing in the meantime.

For all the choices you make on your non-negotiables, show the universe that you mean it by sticking to your decisions. If you meet a guy who doesn't measure up, or you feel you can't be your authentic self, politely let him know you're not interested. This will help the universe send you a guy who does meet your criteria (or something close). And when the time is right, you just might find yourself stumbling into your own happily ever after, just like I did.

CHAPTER 11

Don't Stop Believing

Being in the right head and heart space at the right time is crucial. As you know, I had seen Chris at an event the year before we first made a connection, but he was broken-hearted over his marriage ending, and I apparently needed to deal with one more douchebag. We probably wouldn't have been a great couple if we had gotten together then. Neither of us were in a good place.

So, once we were both in a good place, the universe aligned for us to be together. We were both shocked by how easily things fell into place when we were good with ourselves.

Chris shared with me that he kept seeing the number 420 everywhere. "Are you a pothead?" I jokingly asked him. He laughed and assured me that he wasn't a stoner. It was so weird, but then I started seeing 420 everywhere too. For months, maybe even a whole year, we'd see it multiple times a day. It would be a house number, a license plate, a flight number, an exit off the freeway, a hotel room number, even the time of day on clocks. You name it, we would see it if it had 420 on it. It was out of control. I began studying numerology and found information that it could be angels trying to guide us, but I didn't know to what.

On April 11, 2012, I had a very vivid dream about my grandpa, which wasn't rare, but this dream was different. Chris was standing next to me on the beach, holding my hand. The water was crystal clear and calm. I could see all the beautiful starfish, and we were on the beach where I played with my grandpa as a little girl. It was so peaceful. I was emotional when I woke up and I spoke to my grandpa, hoping he could hear me.

"I wish you could've met him, Grandpa. You would've loved him."

A few days later, on the afternoon of April 14, we went to Whistler, British Columbia, for a weekend getaway and went on a helicopter ride. As I mentioned in the introduction, we were supposed to land on a glacier and have champagne, but it was too icy to land. The pilot circled a few times, and it seemed like there would be no picnic. I was getting dizzy and was just about to suggest that we take this party back to the lodge when Chris pulled out a little black box from his coat pocket. *Is that what I think it is? OMG, it is!*

He took a deep breath and looked at the back of the pilot's head (he told me later he was wishing we were alone on a beautiful glacier like he planned). Next, his hands were shaking as he gently removed the ring from the box. Chris turned to me with a smile on his face and quietly asked, "Will you marry me?"

Of course, I happily accepted, and we both laughed, kissed, and cried tears of joy. It was one of the best moments of my life.

As the helicopter was heading back to the airport I looked down and saw a river running into a frozen-over lake, creating the shape of a heart. I pointed it out to Chris and thought, *How fitting is that?*

The next day, I was updating my calendar on my iPhone, and it dawned on me. Chris happened to propose five years to the day (and at about the same time) of when my grandpa had passed away. Chris would have had no idea of the day or time that my grandfather passed. My grandfather told me a few days before he died that I would find a nice guy. I can't help but feel this was his way of saying, "I told you so," and letting me know he was watching over me. The more open you are to being guided by the universe and your angels, the more these synchronistic things happen.

I realize this may sound crazy, but the synchronicity wasn't. And 420 wasn't done with us, either. We took a trip to Las Vegas, and I remember seeing a beautiful venue that I wanted to book for our wedding. There was an outdoor walkway with waterfalls and palm trees. Then, as 420 continued to show up, Chris said, "If 420 is about angels guiding us then I want to marry my angel on 420." So, we chose April 20 for the wedding ceremony, which was to be held at Valley of the Falls at Mandalay Bay in Las Vegas. The entire process was seamless, and it was going to be our day (with no "What does your mom want?").

Even though it was "our day," my family was very much included. Right before the wedding, my mom sent me an email that said, "Take a look at what I found." It was my grandparents' original wedding certificate. Tears streamed down my face. I couldn't believe what I was reading. They were married on April 20, 1943, in Las Vegas! She also found my grandfather's Air Force badge, and it was numbered 420.

I know my grandfather led Chris and I to each other, and I know he was toasting us on our big day, the same date as his. This was truly a miracle and a sign to show me that I found my Mr. Right.

Some details about our intimate wedding: Our wedding invites were printed on labels which were put on bottles of our favorite wine and delivered to fifty of our closest friends and family. When our guests arrived at our ceremony, a seven-foot-tall Elvis impersonator and his showgirl handed out champagne. Jaide was my maid of honor and Shay (Chris's daughter) stood on his side. We had our reception at the top of Mandalay Bay, overlooking the city lights, and we danced the night away.

We wrote our own vows, and when I look back on all the happy memories of that day, the sharing of our vows is one of my favorite moments. We wrote our vows carefully and with love, and sharing them in front of those closest to us was magical. Here's what we pledged to each other that day:

Chris,

From the beginning, we have shared something incredible that most people dream of. I continue to learn from you and become a better person by knowing you. You have taught me how to love openly and I fall more in love with you every day. You're my best friend, my soul mate, an amazing father, and you make me happier than I could have ever imagined.

I promise to be true to you and always support and love you with all that you do, and will never take you for granted. I promise to stay young at heart, and never let a day go by without letting you know how much I love you. I promise you my heart and soul, my love and compassion, my friendship and trust, I promise you forever. Today is a sign of my faith and commitment to you, Shay, and Jaide. We are now a family, and our journey together begins today.

Stacey,

Marrying you is the easiest decision I have ever made, not because I take the decision lightly, but because I have faith in your honesty, in your integrity and in your affection. I have faith in our love and devotion toward each other and I take you as you are, love you as you are and who you have yet to become. You have the most gorgeous eyes I've ever seen, and your smile can light up a room. But as stunning as you are on the outside, that all pales in comparison to the beauty that you possess on the inside.

You are the warmest, most thoughtful, loving person I have ever met, and I am honored to be able to spend the rest of my life with you. I promise to comfort you, to support you always, and I will celebrate your triumphs and mourn your losses as if they were my own. I promise I will always love you and have faith in your love for me, through all our years and all that life may bring us. I promise my faith and commitment to you, to Jaide, and to Shay. We are now a family, and our journey together begins today.

Those beautiful words of commitment we shared with each other embody everything I'm teaching you in this book. To be able to truthfully mean these words, to say them to someone and be able to hold space to hear them, you have to open your heart to give and receive love. And now I hope your heart is ready to open and let love find you too.

GO INTO SELF-LOVE OVERDRIVE

Becoming your best friend and loving yourself first is the way to find deep, mutual love. I couldn't tell you that until now because you've probably heard some version of that before and thought it was a load of crap. By this point, though, are you more than a little convinced that doing the deep inner work of transforming your emotions and your energy correlates to the outer attraction of who shows up and how they show up for you?

I finally realized the value of spending more time focused on becoming the best version of myself was way better than focusing on finding a man to complete me. When you do the work to get to know yourself and heal your heart from wounds suffered in childhood, or even as recently as your last date, you become a stronger and more loving, lovable you. Have faith that as you do the work, things are happening behind the scenes that you aren't even aware of, like the guidance of 420 was for me. Everything is happening in divine time, so keep focusing on raising your vibration and loving every ounce of yourself.

As you do this work, get in the best shape of your life—not by dieting, but by gaining control over your emotions and healing your past. You'll learn to become your own best friend, and tell yourself what she would tell you, instead of what the "old you" would tell yourself. She also knows what you like and dislike and what you need to declutter— old photos, boxes of love letters in the garage from your ex, etc. She'd gladly spend loads of time hanging out with you and visualizing what it's going to be like when you meet your dream guy.

I will always be committed to doing this work. Yes, I met this amazing guy, but unfortunately the lessons don't stop when your Mr. Right order is filled. Marriage is where the real work starts. That was still just the beginning of my transformation.

Heal Yourself
IT'S TIME TO CREATE YOUR ORDER FOR MR. RIGHT

Now that you have learned that attracting the relationship you truly desire is an inside job, have more clarity around what you want and what you don't want in a relationship, have the ability to spot red flags and know what to do when you see them (a friendly reminder: Run!), know how to heal your past, have acknowledged why it's important to clear the clutter to create space for what you desire, and understand how the universe loves clarity, you're ready to place your order, sister!

How do you place an order for a man? Well, it's just like when you go to a restaurant. You tell the waiter exactly what you want, even if it's vegetarian, gluten-free, lettuce-wrapped, and with a side of extra avocado, delivered exactly how you ordered it, right? You wouldn't walk into a restaurant and tell them to bring you whatever they think you would like. It's the same with the universe. It always sends us what we order, but we're not always consciously ordering, so what we get can include some real douchebags, as we've discussed. When you're clear though, you get the guy you're a match for, the one you really want, because you've done the work to be ready to rock this relationship, graduating from the douchebags to a man worthy of your time.

To create your Mr. Right Order in your journal using notes from Chapter 10, you'll need your favorite pen, a quiet place where you won't be interrupted, and a rose quartz crystal if you have one.

Think about what type of man you would actually want to grow old with. Yes, he can be a millionaire, if that is what you choose is important (no judgment here), but I ask you to please go a little deeper, because when the money's gone or when the relationship gets tough (because they all do at some point), the money won't mean anything to you. This goes for the perfectly fit body as well, because one day that perfectly fit body may not be so perfect. At the end of the day, it's up to you to define for yourself what is important, and this is your opportunity to be clear on that. Dream big, but also think back to your past relationships, about what worked, and what didn't work. Use your past to create an incredible future with someone.

Be intentional with this process. It's important to understand that when we create space in our life for what we truly desire, whether it be literally or energetically, we must declare what we want to fill that space with, to avoid it being filled up with things like drama, or another douchebag. Write the following affirmation in your journal and repeat this affirmation often throughout your day: *I only allow positive vibes in.* This will let the universe know that you only want positive, high-vibe experiences.

Now, in this frame of mind, look at all your notes from Chapter 10 and create your master list. Visualize what your Mr. Right looks like, smells like, dresses like, and feels like. Journal it out. This exercise will help ignite all your senses. Next, write down everything that you want in this Mr. Right order. Be picky! There's no right or wrong here.

Lastly, have fun with this! Allow yourself to daydream about your perfect guy and the relationship the two of you will have. Allow yourself to FEEL how great it's going to be when you're in a relationship with a man who you can trust wholeheartedly. Allow yourself to FEEL how incredible it's going to be, to be in bed with a man who is the furthest thing from selfish. Allow yourself to FEEL how safe you'll feel with him, just knowing how much he loves you for being you.

You'll probably want to come back to this exercise more than once and continue adding to it as you identify more things you want to add to the order and other things you want to exclude or remove. Your Mr. Right order will continue to evolve with you as you do more and more inner work.

After you place your order, act as if it's already happened and BE the energy that you want to attract! How would you live your life? What would you be doing if this man was in your life? How would you dress? How would you speak? Who or what would you let go of in order to create even more space for love and abundance in all areas of your life? What type of friends would you be hanging out with? What types of activities would you be doing? How often would you work out? What would your bedroom be like?

When you can't think of anything else to write, end this process with a Gabby Bernstein quote I love: "I surrender this desire to the Universe. Show me what you got!"

Here are some thoughts I want you to take with you as you move forward and become a match for diamonds, instead of a magnet for douchebags:

- TRUST that things are working out in divine timing.
- TRUST that if a relationship ends, a better one is on the way.
- BELIEVE you are worthy of true love, honesty, respect, and deep connection.
- LOVE every ounce of who you are.
- BE the energy that you want to attract.
- And girl, whatever you do, DO NOT SETTLE.

Conclusion

This is what I know to be true: If you *never* learn how to see emotional triggers as an opportunity for personal growth—especially with relationships—you will always be making life much harder than it really has to be. You'll remain stuck in cycles of unwanted situations, attracting the wrong partner, and never get to live the life that you truly desire. That was certainly the case for me before I learned a lot of the key lessons I've shared in this book, such as:

- The universe was aligning me with people, things, and situations that matched the energy that I was putting out.
- I needed to be open-minded and willing to see things differently if I wanted lasting change and to break the cycle of attracting unhealthy relationships.
- There was wisdom in my wounds.
- I would be loved and respected only as much as I loved and respected myself.
- My inner world was creating my outer world.
- I needed to BE the energy that I wanted to attract.

I went through a lot of douchebags before I finally understood this process and attracted the love of my life. As I mentioned in the introduction to this book, my soul sisters helped me get through the darkest time of my life and I'll be forever grateful, not only for their friendship, but for helping me see the light when I couldn't find it on my own. Unfortunately, this isn't the norm. I hear all too often of women turning their backs on a so-called "friend" during a time when that friend needs that support the most, leaving her to navigate a heartache alone. This is especially challenging if the friend doesn't have someone else to reach out to, or doesn't know who she can trust.

For these reasons and more, I created a private community for readers to come together to share stories, heal, celebrate, and support one another.

To gain access to this sisterhood, or to learn more about working with me directly go to www.staceydewald.com.

Made in the USA
Columbia, SC
06 August 2022

64758382R00078